T0012731

The Unplanned Journey

The Unplanned Journey

Hope, Comfort, and Practical Help for
Parents of Children with Intellectual and
Developmental Disabilities

Janet Kelly

Clovercroft Publishing

The Unplanned Journey: Hope, Comfort, and Practical Help for Parents of
Children with Intellectual and Developmental Disabilities
©2024 Janet Kelly

All rights reserved. No part of this book may be reproduced or transmitted
in any form or by any means, electronic or mechanical, including photocopy-
ing, recording, or by any information storage and retrieval system, without
permission in writing from the copyright owner.

Published by Clovercroft Publishing, Franklin, Tennessee
Clovercroftpublishing.com

Edited by Ann Tatlock

Cover and Interior Design by Suzanne Lawing

Printed in the United States of America

ISBN: 978-1-956370-26-3 (print)

*Sometimes the difficult things that happen
in our lives put us directly on the path to the best
things that will ever happen to us.*
–UNKNOWN

Dedication

To my two beautiful daughters

With love forever,
Your Mama Bear

CONTENTS

INTRODUCTION

At the airport this morning, I heard the unmistakable high-pitched cry of a baby with a neurological disorder. All it took was one glance at the hyper-extending infant to know that the woman pushing the stroller was "one of us"—that is, the parent of a child with special needs. Many years ago I was the one behind the stroller. Part of me wanted to wrap my arms around this woman and tell her everything was going to be okay—eventually. Instead, after returning home, I began writing this book. I wrote it for her, I wrote it for you, and I wrote it as the book I wish someone had written for me.

My guess is that you're already on the receiving end of a lot of philosophical rhetoric these days. Oh, to have a ten-dollar bill for every time someone said to me, "Special babies for special people." And then there were the deniers—I mean, "positive thinkers": "Your girl is going to grow out of this. Just think positive! I've heard that gluten-free diets really help!"

I was in your shoes 31 years ago. I remember the confusion, the fear, the disbelief, and sheer sadness that prevailed in those early days. And that is why I feel so compelled to write to you as someone who has been there. My hope is to be a source of comfort, camaraderie, and practical guidance on your own unplanned journey.

Honestly, had there been a "Most Unlikely to Be Involved with Special Needs Children" award in high school, it probably would have gone to me. Annie Sullivan I'm not, but today I have nothing but gratitude for this unexpected journey I found myself on. You may not be feeling it now, but you've got this; you really do. The truth is that from the time our at-home pregnancy test reads positive, we never know who's preparing to enter our lives. Who doesn't have "special needs" anyway? The key is that you do what you can to nurture all of your children in their greatness—whether they're the next Nobel Peace Prize recipient, local barista, or boy in a wheelchair.

I'm here by your side on this new journey you're on. I'm here to encourage you to grieve, get as much rest as possible, and know that you have no idea how strong and incredible you are.

Janet Kaump Kelly
Louisville, Kentucky
November 22, 2023

CHAPTER ONE

THE DAY MY LIFE CHANGED FOREVER: NOVEMBER 30, 1991

We could never learn to be brave and patient
if there were only joy in the world.
—HELEN KELLER

From my speeding gurney, the words "Emergency C-section!" ricocheted around me. Minutes prior, I had been jolted from sleep by a nurse telling me my baby's heartbeat had gone down to 32 beats per minute and wasn't coming back up. My husband had gone home an hour earlier to take a shower, so I was by myself (other than the team of medical professionals scurrying about). What transpired during the next 30 minutes is still jumbled in my head.

Meanwhile, back home in San Diego's quiet East County, a baby girl's nursery decorated in shades of peaches and cream awaited, complete with a library fit for a future

Pulitzer Prize winner. I had been preparing for this baby's arrival for eight months, and it wasn't just a matter of saying goodbye to Chardonnay and enrolling in Lamaze classes. Doing everything in my power to prevent having a fourth miscarriage, I became a full-on Organic Earth Mama, avoiding everything from nail polish fumes to electromagnetic fields. I'm not sure who was looking forward to meeting this little girl more: my carefree seven-year-old daughter Ann, my engineer husband of 11 years, or my 35-year-old conscientious (okay, slightly obsessive) self.

As my body shook uncontrollably on that gurney, I had no idea that my carefully orchestrated and orderly lifestyle was transforming into a Class 5 hurricane. The living had been easy at 1710 Wingfoot Place. Even Sandy, our nine-year-old golden retriever, followed the rules. The routine rarely varied: Drop Ann off at her private school, head into the office for five hours, pick Ann up, go home, make dinner—you get the picture. Who knew that before the year was over, my parenting journey would take me from alphabetizing the herb and spice jars in my suburban kitchen to poring over medical journals in university libraries.

Now back to that gurney: I cried for joy that November morning when my daughter Kathryn entered the world by emergency C-section. My relieved ob/gyn was happy to tell me that my daughter had survived the ordeal with flying colors, despite the umbilical cord being wrapped tightly around her neck. As I held Kathryn in my arms and looked into her eyes for the first time, however, I felt little of the joy I had experienced upon hearing the doctor's comforting words. Call it mother's intuition or morphine-induced paranoia, but I knew that all was not well with my Kathryn.

As the weeks went by, it became more and more apparent that something indeed was amiss. Kathryn failed to gain weight or make eye contact, and her muscle tone fluctuated from being floppy to overly rigid. Kathryn's seasoned pediatrician, who was also the head of the hospital's neo-natal unit, continued to assure me that she had just gotten off to a slow start and that she'd soon be fine.

I kept telling myself that too, but deep inside, I knew my journey through motherhood had taken an irrevocable turn. After making repeated phone calls to the pediatrician's office to voice my concerns, Kathryn was finally seen by a pediatric occupational therapist four months later. It was just a matter of time before I began hearing terms such as cerebral palsy, autistic-like, and profoundly mentally disabled, but no one could give me an actual diagnosis.

A year later, I revisited Kathryn's pediatrician specifically to ask if he actually did suspect that Kathryn had a problem and was just waiting it out or if he truly didn't see it. He told me he truly didn't see it and that it wasn't the first time he was made wrong by a mother's intuition, and it probably wouldn't be the last.

The bottom line is if you feel there is something off with your baby or child, please seek medical attention as soon (and as often!) as possible until you feel your concerns have been adequately addressed. You can find information on developmental milestones on reputable websites such as CDC.gov. If your baby isn't keeping up with these milestones, such as when they smile for the first time, roll over, take their first step, etc., be sure to let your pediatrician know.

Research indicates that the earlier intervention takes place for your child, the better. The Centers for Disease Control and Prevention (CDC) state that "the connections in a child's brain are most adaptable during the first three years of life. These connections, also called neural circuits, are the foundation for learning, behavior, and health. Over time, these connections become harder to change."[1] By early intervention, I'm referring to such services as:

- Speech-language pathology
- Vision and audiology services
- Occupational and physical therapy
- Early Identification, Intervention Services (EIIS)
- Family training and counseling

Your pediatrician will be able to refer you to whichever services are most appropriate for your child.

CHAPTER TWO

THE DIAGNOSIS

All uncertainty is fruitful . . . so long as it is
accompanied by the wish to understand.
– ANTONIO MACHADO

In my pre-Kathryn days, I was idealistic (or self-righteous?) enough to believe that if you took all the right supplements, thought all the right thoughts, and believed in the right dogma, giving birth to a happy, healthy baby was pretty much a slam dunk. With the health and well-being regimen I was adhering to, surely Kathryn would be the reincarnation of Prima Ballerina Margot Fonteyn. After hearing that my daughter would probably never walk, much less receive a thunderous ovation for a *pas de deux,* my simplistic worldview and any lingering sense of entitlement began to shift a little.

I, who had always thrived upon concrete answers in black-and-white terms, now found myself in support groups where it appeared that everyone but me had concrete answers along with black-and-white terms for their children's conditions: Down syndrome, Fragile X, encephalitis, etc. Meanwhile, Kathryn's neurologist referred to her as "an enigma."

When I was pregnant with my daughter Ann, my favorite book was *What to Expect When You're Expecting*, and after she was born, Penelope Leach's book, *Your Baby & Child From Birth to Age Five* served as my day-by-day playbook. With Kathryn, there was no playbook, and I felt utterly lost.

As misguided as this now sounds, I actually felt a certain measure of relief when Kathryn's pediatrician called to tell me that a blood test revealed that Kathryn had cytomegalovirus (CMV). Despite the disturbing prognosis, at least I had something concrete to hold on to—some explanation to make sense of it all. I quickly contacted the CMV Foundation and began reading everything I could get my hands on about it. Then one evening, Kathryn's pediatrician called to tell us that Kathryn's files had been mixed up with another little girl's. Kathryn did not have CMV, and I was back to my not-so-black-and-white reality.

What I didn't realize at that time was that not every neurological disorder has a name. In Kathryn's case, the umbilical cord was wrapped extremely tightly around her neck, and it was wrapped more times than the ob-gyn had ever witnessed with a live birth. Consequently, there is no name for this. Because some kind of diagnosis must be given for state and federal benefits, Kathryn was finally given a name nonetheless: "Profound mental retardation and cerebral palsy with autistic-like behavior." Years later, "seizure disorder" was added to the mix.

Because of Kathryn's unique facial and body features, she was even seen by one of the nation's leading dysmorphologists for genetic testing. The results came back "normal," just like the results of the genetic testing done after my multiple miscarriages.

Since Kathryn's arrival in 1991, I have seen only one other child who was similar to her. I spotted him while on a tour of an old Amish settlement in southeast Minnesota. Needless to say, the timing wasn't right for me to seek out the mother and ask questions! To this day, I consider Kathryn as my one-of-a-kind miracle.

By now, you are beginning to realize that the term special needs covers an enormous spectrum, and you and your child will have your own specific set of needs. More about this will be covered in the "Resources and Options" section of this book. Also, in this book, I use *IDD, atypical,* and *special needs* interchangeably. All refer to chronic conditions that are due to mental and/or physical impairments.

CHAPTER THREE

A TIME TO GRIEVE

It takes strength to face our sadness and to grieve and to let our grief and our anger flow in tears when they need to. It takes strength to talk about our feelings and to reach out for help and comfort when we need it.
—FRED ROGERS

"Never let 'em see you sweat!" and "The show must go on!" were phrases I heard every day when I was a performing arts student. These phrases were so embedded in my psyche that when Kathryn was born, I was very selective with whom I shared my sadness and disappointment.

While it is wise to be selective when it comes to sharing your deepest emotions, the truth is that the "show" doesn't just go on when you swallow your emotions and carry on as if everything is fine. For those of us who bring an atypical child into the world, we cannot help but feel wounded. And when it comes to any kind of wound, be it physical or emotional, as much as you may want the quick fix, healing runs its own course.

What parent doesn't have hopes and dreams for their child? For some of you, those dreams took root in your own childhood. You may have dreamt of sharing a passion for tennis with your son or visualized fishing trips with your daughter like you had with your mom and dad. In one way or another, you now find yourself experiencing the death of these dreams.

I kept a journal during my pregnancy with Kathryn, and when I was four months pregnant, I wrote,

My Dear Daughter,

Can it really be true? Are you really a girl? It seems too wonderful to be true. Sweetheart, you are so welcome into our family. We love you already and are eager to know you. We will have many special moments, my daughter. You have so much to look forward to—library trips, birthday parties, picking out your own clothes, and going out for frozen yogurt. Together, we will explore the world and discover the gifts God has given you. I love you, my dear daughter.

When you give birth to a child with special needs, it's nearly impossible to visualize your future. Will your daughter be able to walk, talk, or even recognize you? This type of uncertainty can feel overwhelmingly sad and scary. I remember searching desperately for some clues as to what our future might look like. One morning, while waiting at a stoplight, I painfully watched as a haggard-looking woman with empty eyes and faded sweats crossed the street pushing the wheelchair of a head-shaking, arm-flailing little boy I assumed to be her son. Is this what was down the pike for me? What would people see and what judgments would they make as they watched Kathryn and me?

"Look at that poor woman. Do you think she smoked crack during her pregnancy?"

Not that I was any lighter on myself. Considering that only 1–2 percent of the mentally disabled population was classified as profoundly disabled back then, and most of them were males, it was only natural that I asked myself, "What in Sam Hill did I do to cause this?"

For weeks, I mulled over every detail of my pregnancy, scrutinizing my every move, going back to the night of her conception (just how many glasses of champagne *did* I have at cousin Michael's wedding reception that night?) to the day I went bodyboarding off the coast of La Jolla in my early pregnancy. The discomfort of these thoughts was eclipsed by the phrases other people used in an attempt to comfort me:

"Think positive! She'll be fine."

"At least she lived; you must be so grateful for that!"

I quickly learned it wasn't socially acceptable for me to use words like *disappointed* or *sad* to express my feelings.

> *I quickly learned it wasn't socially acceptable for me to use words like disappointed or sad to express my feelings.*

Well-wishers wanted to encourage me with their positive talk and philosophies. At times, I wanted to run down my cul-de-sac shouting, "Doesn't *anybody* think this is sad? Is there not one person who will cry with me instead of trying to be so upbeat?!" But people were uncomfortable that a pregnant woman who neither indulged in daily martinis nor worked in a lead smelter could give birth to a baby who was so profoundly disabled. So, in an effort to maintain order and a sense of concrete answers in their own world, they felt compelled to say things like, "Special babies for special people."

As much as I wanted to take comfort from all the "positivity," it felt more needful and appropriate to mourn the loss of my dream Kathryn—the Kathryn whose outrageously fun slumber parties would echo down the halls of 1710 Wingfoot, the Kathryn who would look like a princess walking down the aisle in her wedding gown, and whose adorable children would one day call me "Grandma." And so, to grieve what felt like a living loss, I retreated into the safe cocoon of my home. Not that I became a raging agoraphobic; I just needed time to avoid the inquiries of strangers ("Have you tried giving her Kombucha?") while not avoiding my brutally honest, albeit brutally messy, feelings of sadness, fear, anger, and confusion (for starters).

> *I feared never having the freedom to go on vacations again, never returning to act onstage, and never being able to walk into a room with my daughter without seeing the look of pity on people's faces.*

I feared never having the freedom to go on vacations

26

again, never returning to act onstage, and never being able to walk into a room with my daughter without seeing the look of pity on people's faces. Most of all, I feared becoming that woman I saw at the crosswalk.

Parenting any newborn can be challenging, but when you bring home a baby with special needs, it can feel like you were planning to run your first 5K, and you've suddenly found yourself dropped off on the Appalachian Trail without a compass, map, cell phone, or backpack.

While everyone grieves differently, it's been my experience that the parents who don't express their feelings to anyone and don't seek help when they're hurting often end up with an unhealed wound that can be just as crippling as any injury in their physical body, if not more. All kinds of complications can appear down the road, including what I refer to as "emotional constipation." I've talked with enough parents who have protective walls around their hearts that rival Ft. Knox. Rather than providing protection, though, these walls have only led to further heartbreak, troubled relationships, and compromised health.

You will be doing yourself and those around you a huge favor if you identify what you're feeling and express it. Uncover what needs to be uncovered, grieve what needs to be grieved, and seek to heal what needs to be healed. Then, and only then, will you be able to move on in a meaningful way toward the goal of acceptance. While you don't need to let everybody see you "sweat," it is in your favor to find at least a few dear souls you can open up to, be it a licensed therapist or your dearest BFF. It's been said that when you share your joy, you double it, and when you share your pain, you cut it in half, and I have found that to be so true.

The worst thing we can do is to stay stuck in our grief. While we must process our grief, it's best to think of it as one episode along our journey. As the author Caroline Myss says, "We are not meant to stay wounded. We are supposed to move through our tragedies and challenges and to help each other move through the painful episodes of our lives. By remaining stuck in the power of our wounds, we block our own transformation . . . We overlook the gifts inherent in our wounds, the strength to overcome them, and the lessons we are meant to receive through them."[2]

The worst thing we can do is to stay stuck in our grief.

Understanding the Kubler-Ross Five Stages of Grief Model[3] was a tremendous help to me as Kathryn's mom. Each of these stages applies to the stages of emotional pain that we parents with a special needs child go through:

- Denial

- Anger

- Bargaining/seeking to control or fix everything

- Depression and isolation

- Acceptance

Before we look at each stage, know that not everyone may experience every single one of them, and the first four stages don't necessarily follow the order above. You may experience anger first, and then denial or depression, and then go straight into bargaining. You may experience all these stages within a week or you may spend years stuck in one stage. The important thing is that you recognize where you and your loved ones are as you move forward with your child's care.

This is helpful if you are in full-blown "Let's fix this!" mode and your spouse is in total denial because it clarifies how there can be conflicts or distance within your relationship. Giving a name to these different stages can help you to approach the situation with greater understanding, empathy, and love. Getting to acceptance and to a place where you and your child are thriving is a process, and processing all the emotions in these stages is a significant part of it.

CHAPTER FOUR

NAVIGATING THROUGH THE STAGES OF GRIEF

In the depth of winter, I finally learned that there was in me an invincible summer.
–ALBERT CAMUS

DENIAL

I have a T-shirt that says, "Denial is my happy place." I thought it was funny when I bought it, but the truth is that denial may seem like a happy place at first, but it's only putting off the inevitable, i.e., getting appropriate care for your child.

It's only natural that we welcome denial whenever we are avoiding pain. But growth oftentimes requires pain. As Richard Paul Evans said in *The Walk,* "Some people go to such lengths to avoid pain that they give up on life. They bury their hearts, or they drug or drink themselves numb until they don't feel anything anymore. The irony is, in the end their escape becomes more painful than what they're avoiding."[4]

Nevertheless, sometimes denial can be your friend for a season when it's actually serving as a protective defense mechanism. Sometimes you can only take in so much at one time.

Please remember that you are only human and you deserve just as much compassion and gentle care as your child does.

Please remember that you are only human and you deserve just as much compassion and gentle care as your child does. If you need to be in denial for a little while, so be it. What you're experiencing is 100% natural and to be expected.

ANGER

It's entirely understandable that you're angry. It helps to know that typically anger comes from fear, and I don't need to list all the scenarios that might be causing you fear right now. You might be fearful of how this is going to affect your marriage or what other people might think of you, or your anger might simply be because you are the quintessential mama (or papa) bear protecting your cub.

Unprocessed anger is one of those emotions that can sometimes come out sideways out of nowhere. Anger has never really been part of my natural temperament, so one day when I did fly off the handle with a complete stranger, it served as a powerful red flag that I was hurting and had some work to do! On that particular afternoon, Kathryn had an important appointment with a pediatric neurologist. I parked in a handicapped parking space, but in my haste, I forgot to hang my placard. I hadn't even unbuckled Kathryn from her car seat when a woman began spewing hateful words about me: "What kind of woman would take a handicapped spot at a hospital when she's young and healthy?!" I carried Kathryn over to her and shouted, "Is this handicapped enough for you? Does profound brain damage count?" I can't even express how out of character this type of outburst was for me. And THAT is what I mean by anger sometimes coming out "sideways." Watch for it, and when it happens, know you are not alone.

While anger is absolutely appropriate during this phase of grieving, it is important that you not let it sabotage getting help for your child. Name it, feel it, and express it with appropriate loved ones and qualified health care professionals, but do try to leave it at the door when interacting on your child's behalf. It is crucial that you work together as a team with your child's entourage of health professionals. The best way to accomplish this is to respectfully communicate your desires concerning your child's care while leaving anger out of the equation.

As an example, for whatever reason, people tended to refer to my daughter Kathryn by anything but her given name. Every time I heard "Kathy" or "Katrina," I would cringe and want to scream, "HER NAME IS KATHRYN. What part of Kathryn do you not understand?!" At a time when so many details concerning my daughter's future were completely out of my control, at least her name was something I felt I should be able to control. And so, when even this area felt out of control, I felt angry. Would it have helped for me to lose my cool with people over this though? I think not. Early on, I learned the wisdom in choosing my battles.

As my mother always used to say, "You win more bees with honey," and I found this to be very true when it came to my daughter's care. Yes, you must be your child's unwavering advocate, but it always works in your favor to come from a calm and respectful place. The bottom line is that you should never back down from fighting for what your child needs, but communicating from a place of vitriol is not an effective strategy. If you're not able to get the resources and services your child needs, seek help higher up in whatever organization you're dealing with, or if necessary, hire an attorney or a professional advocate.

From a health standpoint, anger can elevate your blood pressure, cause cardiac issues, affect your immune system, and when sustained, it can shorten your very life. Needless to say, it doesn't do any favors for your relationships or the well-being of your children either. On the flip side, let your anger lead you to action– not only action in terms of helping your child, but don't forget yourself either (more about that in Chapter Ten, "A Time for Joy and Perpetual Self Care!").

Hand in hand with anger is blame. Part of feeling fearful and out of control leads you to blame other people, other things, and even yourself for your child's issues. You constantly question your decisions, and you'll blame everything from vaccines to pollution to parabens. Again, it's understandable, but ultimately, it is not helpful. Rather than zeroing in on blaming yourself or anyone else, seek to find solutions for helping yourself and your child.

The most important thing is that you never take out your anger on your child. Ever. Go to therapy, take anger management classes, take a run in the park, join a gym for regular workouts, practice self-care, strive to use your anger to fuel positive productivity, and don't forget to b-r-e-a-t-h-e.

> *Please allow your anger phase to be your launching pad, not your final destination.*

Anger can be a tremendous motivator, but not if you get stuck in it. Nothing can transform you into becoming a perpetual victim like being stuck in anger mode. Please allow your anger phase to be your launching pad, not your final destination.

BARGAINING/SEEKING TO CONTROL OR "FIX" EVERYTHING

Welcome to where I hung out for years during my process! For my journey, I pretty much skipped steps 1 (Denial) and 2 (Anger) and went straight to a brief period of depression and isolation before going straight into "fix it" mode.

Unwilling to accept the "Kathryn-is-an-enigma" diagnosis, I set out to read everything I could on brain injuries, neurological syndromes, and childhood disorders. (In pre-Google days, this was some walk in the microfiche park!)

Still finding no answers, I endeavored to "fix" my Enigma Girl anyway. I immersed myself in the world of therapies—

physical, occupational, water, cranial-sacral, vision, senso-rimotor—trying anything that even remotely held promise. Unfortunately, all this had a greater impact on our savings account than on our daughter. Of course, you'll always want to be aware of new advances pertaining to your child's condition, but I'm talking about those signs that you are obsessed with fixing your child at the detriment of your own health and well-being.

During this stage in my journey, I would hold out hope for this therapist or that expert. It was like I was always "off to see the Wizard." If I could just get Kathryn in to see Dr. So-and-so, she'll be able to identify what's wrong and fix it! Accepting the status quo and living with uncertainty just wasn't in my DNA.

After reading about healing through birth reenactments, I even had a good friend sew a replica of a womb, complete with fabric placenta and umbilical cord. Together, we reenacted Kathryn's birth in order to hopefully bring some semblance of emotional healing for her. As Kathryn began to play with the cord inside the womb, I lovingly said, "You don't need to wrap that around your neck this time, Kathryn. There you go. You're doing just fine," as we guided her down the fabric birth canal, all while listening to Pachelbel's Canon. (I played Pachelbel's Canon regularly while pregnant because of studies I read on the positive effects of prenatal exposure to it.) I'm telling you—I was willing to try just about anything if it meant helping Kathryn be all she could be.

I eventually came to the realization that while I could shower Kathryn with love and see that her needs were being met, I couldn't fix her. This didn't mean she couldn't fix me, however. More about that in Chapter Fourteen, "Lessons I Learned from Kathryn."

The most important gift you can give your child is to "get" them. With atypical children (and with all children, really), there is no "one size fits all" guidebook. Your primary goal is to figure out how your child's mind works and to see the world the way they see

> *The most important gift you can give your child is to "get" them.*

it. Does your child crave being securely held or does he recoil from any form of touch? Does her heart sing when listening to music, or does she cover her ears whenever music comes on the radio? It doesn't matter what the parenting books or your best friend advises you to do; it is up to you to understand the unique needs of your child and to communicate those needs with her team of professionals. Together, as a team, you will develop the most effective ways to address your child's needs.

DEPRESSION

If you experience depression at some point in your journey with your child, you are not alone. There will be times when you feel defeated, exhausted, and completely burned out. As someone who has been there, I first want to validate your feelings, but I also want to give you hope. As trite as this may sound in the moment, the truth is that the overwhelming sadness you may be experiencing right now will pass.

For me, I think I was more in denial regarding my depression than I was regarding my child's disability! I somehow felt that if I admitted to being depressed, I would be letting my child down or admitting weakness or failure.

Depression truly is a phase, though. Just as nature has its distinct seasons, there are "seasons" to this journey you're on. It's only natural that at some point, you will experience "wintertime." But here's the gift: While winter's bare branches may not look pretty at first, they actually have their own unique beauty, especially when they reveal amazing views that are otherwise blocked during the other seasons. Having a child with special needs will open your eyes in a way you never knew possible, and you will begin to see beauty in the most unexpected places.

Having a child with special needs will open your eyes in a way you never knew possible, and you will begin to see beauty in the most unexpected places.

Also, what you don't see during the bleakness of winter is the new life preparing to bloom. That's the magic of winter. You never really know what's going on under the surface of the earth. For those of you who find yourself in the wintertime of your life, be assured that dormancy and hibernation don't last forever. If you're brave enough to fully experience these times of darkness, the clarity and vision you'll gain will bring about a renewal you won't believe.

Please don't lose sight that there are other seasons coming. In the meantime, take comfort in knowing that there's nothing like hibernation for pondering some of the questions your new journey asks of you, such as "What is it that I would *like* to feel as opposed to feeling angry, sad, or hopeless?" and "What modifications can I make so that both my child and I can thrive?"

You can either let winter do its work, having your dormant bulbs transform into beautiful flowers as you reinvent your way of being, or you can choose to insulate yourself with distractions, denial, and busyness while remaining stuck in your current frame of mind.

As scary as depression may seem, I encourage you to challenge yourself to go deep during this time while never losing sight that a new day *is* coming. Some strategies I found helpful during these times were to:

Monitor your self-talk. One of my favorite coffee mugs says, "Change your thinking, change your world." It's so true. The next time some catastrophic thought pops into your head, pause, and then reframe that thought. As an example, I used to have a fear that I would pass away before Kathryn and no one would go see her, and her life would fall apart because I wouldn't be there to make important decisions for her. To change that thought, I would reframe it like this: "Kathryn will always be taken care of. On Monday I will call her social worker to ask how to get the ball rolling for my daughter Ann to become her legal conservator upon my passing."

Did you know that humans are the only species who grieve abstract loss? In other words, there are animals who grieve the death of their owner or another animal they were close to, but only we humans grieve over what *could* have been or what *might* be coming down the road for us. I just shared with you one of my abstract fears. What are yours? How can you reframe them?

Monitor your focus. I'll always remember when I was at the San Diego Zoo on a picture-perfect day. While breathing in all the outrageous beauty around me, I overheard a woman getting all huffy because she wasn't seeing enough animals. She said she was going to "write a letter." I told this woman that the best time for seeing animals was either early in the morning or after 3:00 p.m. She said she was still going to write a letter to the management because it just wasn't right. I had no way of knowing if perhaps she had just traveled a long distance and spent her last dollar to see the animals at the world famous San Diego Zoo, or if perhaps she had just arrived after having a root canal.

But I did leave that encounter with greater insight into how our focus determines what we see, feel, and experience. The bottom line is that experiencing disappointment is part of the human experience. Not everyone who buys a Mega Millions ticket wins, not every ballerina makes the Joffrey Ballet, and not every pregnant woman who eats all organic food and never misses an ob-gyn appointment is promised a healthy baby. That's just the way it is. I remember days of parenting young Kathryn when I would have loved to write a letter to management, had there been one. The reality of that woman's time at the zoo was that despite her feelings of outrage about the absent animals, she was actually surrounded by incredibly good things. She just needed to see them! Although she couldn't control the animals' actions, she could control what she focused on. As I began shifting my thoughts from what wasn't "right" about the situation with my daughter to all the good I could see around me, from my refrigerator stocked with nutritious food to my daughter's infectious giggle, I began to feel my stress dissolve. I know this probably sounds Pollyannaish, but it works.

The next time you have an "I'm going to write a letter!" moment, please remember to be gentle on yourself, let the moment pass, decide to do something differently, or to look at the situation in a different way. One of my inspirational heroes is Viktor Frankl, author of *Man's Search for Meaning*. Despite experiencing the atrocities of four different concentration camps in Nazi Germany, he came to the conclusion that "Everything can be taken from a man but one thing: the last of human freedoms – to choose one's attitude in any given set of circumstances, to choose one's way."[5] Now that is inspiration.

Meditate/Pray. You've undoubtedly heard about countless studies supporting the benefits of meditation. These science-based studies show that meditation can do everything from reduce anxiety and depression to improve your sleep. So why are some of us so reluctant to do it? As someone who put off meditating for years (more like decades, really), I'll share with you what helped me to finally get on the meditation bandwagon.

Basically, I stopped complicating it, thinking that I had to do it "right" by using proper mantras or sitting just so in a lotus position for an hour. Yes, you can take classes and go to retreats or watch meditation experts on YouTube, but let me make it simple for you the way a friend made it simple for me.

- Simply find a quiet place in your home where you can sit down, preferably on a cushion on the floor with your back straight, but if the only way you're going to start meditating is from your La-Z-Boy, by all means, settle in on that recliner!

- Set your timer for three to five minutes. (I started with three and now usually do five.)

- Focus on your breath. Inhale deeply through your nose so your belly expands. Now exhale deeply through your nose or mouth, counting slowly to five as you exhale.

- Repeat until your timer goes off.

That's it! I guarantee that if you do this every day until it's a habit, you will benefit from the practice so much that you'll wonder how you ever got by without it!

Please don't complicate this. If your mind becomes distracted while meditating, simply return to your breath as your anchor. You may also find that saying a simple mantra may help. On the in breath, you can think "I breathe in peace" (or joy or calm or whatever resonates with you), and on the out breath, think "I exhale all stress" (or disappointment, anger, or whatever is needed in your present moment). Prayer is a personal decision, but because my faith is very important to me, I begin each morning with five minutes of prayer, and then move on to five minutes of meditation. I feel like it's the best spent 10 minutes of my day.

Make something good happen that has nothing to do with your child. When Kathryn was maybe three years old, I decided to purposefully seek out easy projects that would make me feel like I was accomplishing something aside from parenting. I started by entering my cookies in the California State Fair each year. It's crazy how good it felt to win a red second place ribbon. Then I took a once-a-week art class in my neighborhood, and when Kathryn was four, I volunteered with around 100 other women to learn a Hip-Hop dance routine that was performed at San Diego's former Jack Murphy Stadium for the American Lung Association's fundraiser.

These "projects" that were just for me made all the difference for my mental health and well-being. What might be some feel-good projects for you?

It's so important to give yourself permission to take a break!

It's so important to give yourself permission to take a break! There was a time when I pretty much viewed myself solely as "Kathryn's mom," and I lost sight of the woman I was apart from my daughter. This can put you in a very vulnerable spot, particularly if you are married. This is why I highly recommend finding something that interests you and going for it, be it a one-time event or a once-a-week activity.

Cultivate a tribe. It is in your child's (as well as your own) best interest to be part of a community, whether it's your extended family, parenting support group, church, synagogue, mosque, or cultural group. Even social networks like Facebook and Instagram can be beneficial when used in a positive way. Research suggests that people with meaningful relationships are healthier and happier. Whether you get together for coffee with a friend every weekend or schedule a phone call with an out-of-town buddy, any investment of time is beneficial when it comes to nurturing relationships.

It is important to note that clinical depression is not the same as depressive feelings that are caused by loss or bereavement.[6] If you are experiencing any of the following, you may have clinical depression and I beg you to please seek help:

- Loss of interest in activities you once enjoyed
- Significant weight loss or gain
- Insomnia or excessive sleeping
- Difficulty making decisions
- Lack of energy
- Thoughts of suicide

I cannot stress enough that there is absolutely no shame in seeking the help you so deserve. If you or a loved one should ever think about harming yourself in any way, you can call or text 988 to reach the Suicide & Crisis Lifeline. You will reach a trained counselor who will listen to you and provide resources and support.

If they feel you are in danger, they will discuss connecting you to your local emergency services through 911, but first they will do everything they can to help you before going that route.

Lastly, remember that time (and plenty of restorative sleep and good nutrition!) is sometimes the best medicine. Go easy on yourself, and continue to tell yourself: "This too shall pass."

CHAPTER FIVE

ACCEPTANCE

Motherhood is about raising—and celebrating—the child you have, not the child you thought you'd have. It's about understanding that he is exactly the person he is supposed to be. And, if you're lucky, he just might be the teacher who turns you into the person you're supposed to be.
–JOAN RYAN, *The Water Giver*

I had a friend who once said, "Nothing good ever came out of the Easy-Bake Oven." The same can be said for cultivating "acceptance." There is no FastPass, and I offer no blueprint for getting to the acceptance stage. Again, time is on your side. Over time, you will be so accustomed to your new normal that one day you will wake up and realize that you are indeed in the "acceptance" mode. Over time, we invariably adapt to where our child is at in life.

It reminds me of when I moved to a house near the trolley tracks. At first, every time that trolley raced past my house, I would be startled. In time, I didn't even hear it. The same can be said for parenting your atypical child.

Slowly but surely you adapt to your journey with them. Remember how much we disliked the masks we all wore in the thick of the COVID pandemic? How many of you got so used to wearing them that they just became part of your daily routine?

Acceptance also isn't the be-all and end-all. It isn't some sort of finish line, and it's not a fixed position. You can have days where you go right back to anger or depression. Your unplanned journey is just that—unplanned.

All I know is that one day I noticed that I no longer saw Kathryn's disability. Yes, she still had impossibly matted hair from constantly shaking her head back and forth in her chair, and two missing front teeth from the time she fell face first on a tile floor, and eyes that went in two separate directions from her strabismus, but that was just her, just as much as my other daughter's dry sense of humor, tremendous physical strength, and gorgeous green eyes were *her*. Both daughters were one of a kind. I no longer expected Kathryn to one day say "Mama" any more than I expected my non-huggy daughter Ann to burst into the room and give me a big ol' bear hug just because.

As their mom, I learned to be happy that they were happy. Neither of them needed to adhere to my preconceived notions of what the perfect daughters would be. In a perfect world, would I be elated that at least one of them wanted to hug their exceedingly touchy-feely mom? You bet! But none of us are doing our children any favors expecting them to be the way we want them to be. In reality, both of my daughters were born perfectly imperfect, just as you and I came into the world perfectly imperfect. The sooner we can accept that, the happier we will be.

When I look back on Kathryn's life, there was a defining moment of acceptance that stands out above all the rest. This past March, I was sitting next to a woman on the plane after we flew from San Diego to Chicago. After landing, the woman asked me what had brought me to San Diego, and I told her I was visiting my daughter. I left out the part that I had been at her bedside in the hospital for eight days while she was recovering from a mastectomy. I also didn't mention that she had profound special needs, terminal cancer, or COVID. Nope, to her, I was just a nice woman who was visiting her daughter in beautiful San Diego. She exclaimed that she too had been visiting her daughter in San Diego to celebrate her doctorate. As I commented on how proud she must be, the thought popped into my head that she couldn't possibly be more proud of her daughter than I was of mine.

Now, this was not typical self-talk for me! Typically, these types of dialogues would leave me feeling a little blue. Sure, I always felt happy for people whose adult children were excelling in life, but a little sadness would invariably creep into my psyche as I'd envision Kathryn grabbing gummy bears as her form of self actualization.

This time it was different. After spending so much time with Kathryn and watching her persevere through an absolutely nightmarish hospital stay, she became a full-on rock star to me. I still can barely think of that week without getting teared up. While I had felt a certain measure of acceptance before, these new emotions surpassed that. This was the day I realized I could not be more proud of my daughter, gummy bear grabbing and all.

So much about my parenting journey has consisted of "letting go." Having a child with special needs is the ultimate test in letting go, so in that sense, I couldn't have asked for a better teacher than Kathryn. I wonder what powerful lessons are in store for you.

I eventually learned that I couldn't control a thing. I couldn't even control whether people called my daughter Kathryn, Kathy, or Katrina. What I could control, however, were my choices, so I chose to seek joy and make myself the best person I could be while assuring my daughter's needs were met. This to me is acceptance.

On Children
by Kahil Gibran

They come through you but not from you,
And though they are with you, yet they belong not to you.
You may give them your love but not your thoughts.
For they have their own thoughts.
You may house their bodies but not their souls. [7]

CHAPTER SIX

RESOURCES AND OPTIONS

The best advice I can give to anyone going through a rough patch is to never be afraid to ask for help.
–DEMI LOVATO, *Staying Strong*

When you first find yourself floundering in the Sea of Special Needs, you may feel like you're drowning. You may feel like your ship has sunk and you can't even see the shoreline, but I promise you it's there. You're just going to need some new resources. Bring on the life preservers, life rafts, lifelines, and maybe even an island or two. Welcome to the Resources and Options section that will help you make it to shore and assist your child in living his or her best life.

You'll want to collect information about your child's disability from every good source you can, beginning with your child's pediatrician. Another great resource is the Center for Parent Information and Resources (CPIR). Their website is ParentCenterHub.org. They offer information and connections to the full spectrum of disabilities in children, including developmental delays and rare disorders. On their site, you can find links to learn about typical developmental milestones in childhood as well as information on identifying and treating specific disabilities and disorders.

You may find out about your local resources by asking your pediatrician or visiting Childcare.gov and checking out your state's resources. Some of the resources available are childcare, health and social services, financial assistance, and more.

EDUCATION

Each state is required by federal law to provide children with special needs a free and appropriate public education under the Individuals with Disabilities Education Act (IDEA).

Educational services can include special education classes, therapy services, and assistive technology devices. These services can help children with special needs reach their full potential and succeed to the best of their ability in school. Once you make contact with your local social services, you will be assigned a social worker who will be an invaluable resource for you and your child. She can inform you of early intervention services in your area for children from birth to age three as well as organizations such as Autism, Cerebral Palsy, Down Syndrome Societies, and many more.

When your child turns three, he will receive an Individualized Education Program (IEP). An IEP team will be assigned, and your child's IEP will be reviewed on an annual basis. Of course, you will be involved every step of the way!

Keep in mind that as your child gets older, there are wonderful day programs that may provide many growth opportunities for your young adult from community service to positions within the local workforce, and even arts and crafts and the performing arts. Kathryn loved the day program she was in as an adult. I think it gave her a comforting feeling of routine as well as just the right amount of stimulation.

The Arc is a disability rights organization that works with and for people with IDD (intellectual or developmental disability), their families, and their communities. They use the power of advocacy to improve the lives of people with IDD. You can check their website for chapters in each state at www.thearc.org.

THERAPIES

Your pediatrician will be able to recommend the best form of therapy or therapies for your baby or child. For example, if a baby has a hearing loss, he would be eligible for speech and language therapy. With all therapies, the sooner you begin, the more beneficial it is.

PHYSICAL THERAPY (PT)

PT is invaluable for babies who suffered any form of trauma at birth. If your baby has low muscle tone or is slow in sitting, crawling, standing, or walking, PT may be recommended. Physical therapists are involved with exercising and strengthening the large muscles of the body. When your baby goes to a physical therapist, they will demonstrate exercises for you to do with your baby at home as well.

Kathryn's physical therapist worked with her a lot on walking, and at age 12, she took her first steps. PT continued to work with her on this, as did her school staff, and the caregivers in her group home. Just because Kathryn was physically able to walk didn't mean she wanted to though. Kathryn loved her wheelchair (and all chairs, really), and unless there was food or a car ride involved, getting her out of a sitting position was no small feat!

OCCUPATIONAL THERAPY (OT)

Prior to Kathryn's birth, I thought OT provided career assistance to the unemployed. In reality, OT is used to help anyone from babies to adults with fine motor skills, coordination, and other critical skills challenges to help them perform basic tasks from eating to grasping cups and pencils. For babies and children with severe developmental delays, the occupational therapist helps them with a wide range of activities, from tolerating being in certain positions to playing with toys.

An OT is also a good resource to advise you regarding any adaptations you may need to make to your home. They can assess whether your doorways are wide enough to accommodate your child's wheelchair, and they can even arrange for your door frames to be widened. If your child is prone to falling, an OT or PT can provide resources for floor mats as well as helpful medical adaptations for the bathroom such as wall-mounted shower stools, handrails, and grab bars. Medicaid may cover some of these expenses when they are ordered by a doctor.

SUPPLEMENTAL SECURITY INCOME (SSI)

You will want to check out benefits for your child with the Social Security Administration. Depending upon the severity of your child's disability and other factors, he may be eligible for financial help, even as a baby. For contact information and application procedures, you can visit their website at www.ssa.gov. Your social worker will also be able to provide you with more information regarding this.

RESPITE CARE PROGRAMS

Also of great benefit are respite care programs. They provide short-term and even overnight care that allows you some relief. Most children with a disability qualify for home and community-based Medicaid waivers that cover the cost of respite care. We had the most wonderful respite care providers come to our home once a week to provide me with a morning or afternoon to myself. In the beginning it can be hard to leave your child, but taking time away from them can be so beneficial not only for yourself, but for your child too!

If I could go back in time, I would have used my respite breaks to go for more walks on the beach (we lived in San Diego, so what was I thinking?) or more time with friends. Instead, what I did back in those days was to use nearly all my respite time to go to university libraries to research brain damage and medical disorders!

Remember, you deserve a break. Please do as I say and not as I did. In order to take the best possible care of your child, you must take care of yourself. Your whole world seems brighter when you are rested and refreshed. For information on respite care in your state, visit the ARCH (National Respite Network) website: https://archrespite.org/.

FIND A ROLE MODEL FOR YOUR CHILD

For children who are higher functioning, it is so valuable to find an adult with the same or similar diagnosis as your child's.[8] For instance, if your child has Down syndrome, it is so beneficial for them to meet an adult with Down syndrome. Your social worker may be able to assist you with this or point you in the right direction. You may also check websites of organizations that represent your child's needs.

Another idea is to seek out celebrities on TV or social media who have similar disabilities as your child. Exposing your child to others who have gone on to lead fulfilling and productive lives can be very inspirational. The Disabled World website provides information on famous people with disabilities: www.disabled-world.com.

Exposing your child to the Special Olympics provides another great opportunity for inclusion as well as inspiration. Their website provides all the information you need: www.SpecialOlympics.org.

COMMUNITY CARE FACILITIES/GROUP HOMES FOR CHILDREN

When Kathryn was around eight years old, we placed her in a very loving state-funded group home, which is another option for you.

Because neither her father nor I was able to provide around-the-clock care for her after going our separate ways, this option made the most sense for us.

Each state has its own set-up, and these arrangements may be called residential care facilities, community care facilities, or group homes. All are basically group homes that provide 24-hour nonmedical residential care to children with intellectual/developmental disabilities who need personal services, supervision, and/or assistance essential for self-protection or sustaining the activities of their daily living.

When researching the right group home for your child, you'll want to consider location, the look and feel of the home, how long they have been in operation, and how long they plan on staying in operation, the overall vibe of the residents, and perhaps most importantly, the rapport you have with the care provider and staff. Are you on the same page with them regarding expectations and core values? What kind of meals are served? Do they take regular trips out into the community? What other group activities do they do? Talk with others about the home–your medical professionals, your child's school, etc.

In Kathryn's particular group home, she was able to live there for her entire life. The woman whose home served as the care facility was the care provider, and she welcomed us all as family. Ann and I visited often, and Kathryn was immensely happy there. She was dearly loved by the entire staff, and it truly was her home.

ADOPTION

Placing your baby for adoption may be another loving option. This may sound rather off-putting for some of you, and some of you may wonder why I would even include a section about this in my book. One of Kathryn's greatest gifts to me was that along my own journey, I learned not to judge other parents' decisions because I hadn't walked in their shoes. Truly, that's the main message I want to convey in this book, that you have options and choices, and that nobody has the right to judge what makes sense for you.

Parents who give birth to babies with medical, developmental, or other special needs are just as diverse as the babies themselves. You might be a single dad with four young children at home or a mom with emotional issues that might limit your ability to provide your child with the time and attention they will need. It really doesn't matter what your situation is; you know your story. Years ago, I met a very career-minded younger couple who chose to place their three-year-old son with special needs for adoption. That son of theirs was adopted by a very loving older couple in another state, and I've heard they are all thriving today. When any decision is made with the intention of providing a better life for a child, who are any of us to judge?

The good news is that there are people out there who would love to provide your baby with the love, attention, and finances in which he or she can thrive. If you would like to explore this option, talk with your doctor, social worker, or your local Planned Parenthood health center. They can refer you to trusted adoption agencies in your area.

Again, you are in control. You will be able to choose the type of adoption that feels like the right fit for you. You may want to choose your baby's adoptive parents, you may want to remain in contact with your child and adoptive family, or you may prefer a closed adoption. It is all up to you.

What helps some parents is to talk with others who have chosen adoption for their child. Undoubtedly, the decision to place your baby for adoption will be one of the most difficult and life-altering decisions of your life, so please go easy on yourself, nurture yourself, and give yourself time to heal.

CHAPTER SEVEN

MEDICAL CONCERNS

The good physician treats the disease; the great physician treats the patient who has the disease.
–WILLIAM OSLER

CHOOSING A PEDIATRICIAN

The pediatrician you chose before your child's birth may no longer be the best fit for your child with special needs. Talk with other parents and research online for a physician who is comfortable and competent dealing with whatever disability your child has. The American Academy of Pediatrics (www.aap.org) offers a free online service for parents to find appropriate doctors in their geographical location. Information you will want to know is:

- What is the doctor's specialty?

- Is the doctor accepting new patients?

- What insurance is accepted?
- Which hospital(s) does the doctor serve?

Once you've identified some possible candidates, ask if you can schedule a consultative appointment. It is important that you see how the doctor interacts with your child as well as with yourself, so be sure to bring your child along to the appointment.

MEDICATION

If your child is on medications, you will want to keep a daily medicine log near where you store your medications. Whether you take turns with your spouse or other helper to give your child meds or if your brain is sleep deprived or on overdrive, a log is the best way to keep everything straight. When it comes to your child's medications, you can't afford to make any mistakes! You can make your own log or find a free printable one online. Pinterest has some great ones! You'll want your log to list all of your child's medications along with the dosage, instructions, and any specific notes. You'll need boxes or blanks where you can fill in the time each dose is given. If you prefer, you can write when each dose is due each day and then cross it off as you give it. On your log, it's also a good idea to list any important phone numbers such as physicians, your pharmacy, etc.

RESEARCH HOSPITALS IN YOUR AREA

Kathryn always received the best care at our local children's hospital. Most large metropolitan areas have a children's hospital, and you can do an online search for one near you at www.childrenshospitals.net. If you are close to a Shriners Children's hospital, all of their services are free of charge. Many large hospitals also have Ronald McDonald Houses where they offer free lodging, meals, and a place for children to attend school away from home.

Whenever you check in to a hospital or emergency room, having all your medical information with you is invaluable. I never left home without a copy of all of Kathryn's medical information with me. Of course you'll want to have a copy of this accessible in your home as well for anyone who is caring for your child. The American College of Emergency Physicians and the American Academy of Pediatrics have created an Emergency Information Form for Children with Special Health Care Needs. You can download this form from their website: www.acep.org. Having this document with you will assure that your child will receive the most prompt and appropriate medical care possible.

DENTAL CARE

You will be best served by finding a dentist experienced with special needs children. You can use the www.aap.org website (American Academy of Pediatrics) to locate an appropriate dentist for your child. For children who are high functioning, you can read them books about visiting the dentist and you can even play dentist, using one of your child's dolls or stuffed animals.

In Kathryn's case, she needed to be under general anesthesia for even simple cleanings and check-ups.

ALTERNATIVE MEDICINE

Also referred to as "complementary" or "integrative" medicine, these labels refer to anything from acupuncture to TCM (Traditional Chinese Medicine).

As parents, it is so tempting to try anything that offers some promise that it will help our child. This can make us vulnerable to health frauds and quackery. Even the most intelligent and well-educated individuals have fallen prey to spending copious amounts of time and money on procedures and supplements, only to discover they are completely ineffectual.

With that said, I did try quite a few modalities that were considered alternative when Kathryn was young. Some medical professionals feel that craniosacral therapy is "quackery," but I felt it was beneficial for Kathryn in that she always seemed more "with it" after treatments. A Doctor of Osteopathy (D.O.) provided the treatments, and I learned a lot about nutrition and homeopathy from him. When Kathryn still lived at home, she really responded well to homeopathy, but again, most medical professionals consider it pseudoscience vs. science-based medicine.

My recommendation is to do your due diligence by being an informed consumer. Research scientific studies on whatever product or practice that interests you. I have found that The National Center for Complementary and Integrative Health website, https://www.nccih.nih.gov/, is a very credible source. This is an official website of the United States Government. Of course you will want to run any supplements by your child's pediatrician or neurologist before giving them to your child.

Another resource is Quackwatch.org, a website that focuses on health frauds, fads, trends, and fallacies. Through them, you can also find a large library of legal cases and regulatory actions against questionable medical products.

CHAPTER EIGHT

CAUTION: ROAD BUMPS AHEAD!

No one can make you feel inferior without your consent.
—Eleanor Roosevelt

YOUR RELATIONSHIPS

After you receive some form of a diagnosis, you may want or need to share this information with family, friends, and others. Unfortunately, sometimes even your dearest friends and family members are not equipped to deal with such news. When I expressed my disappointment and fears to my best friend at the time, she told me I must stay positive. While there are times to be a cheerleader for a friend, this was a time when I needed her to cry with me. Sadly, our friendship did not survive.

Maybe your best friend has been your spouse? It is imperative that you prioritize your marriage like never before.

Surveys show that the divorce rate in families with a child with disabilities is as high as 87%. For families with a child with autism, the divorce rate is about 80%.[9] Just as I changed during this journey, so did our marriage. Because Kathryn's very life opened me up to feeling so deeply and to facing reality head-on rather than living in a bubble of "safe and pleasant" denial, I came to terms with my failing marriage and eventually filed for divorce when Kathryn was five years old.

It is imperative that you prioritize your marriage like never before.

A FEW WORDS REGARDING DIVORCE

Choosing divorce when you have a child with special needs should be a last resort. While I ultimately do not regret my decision to divorce, it did complicate life immensely. Remember the analogy I used about having a child with special needs is like finding yourself on the Appalachian Trail without a compass, map, cell phone, or backpack? Well, now let's add the howling of wolves in the distance and bear tracks in the mud—mud that you're trudging in because of the thunderous rainstorm that just drenched your clothes. In short, sometimes divorce is not as easy as you think it will be. Needless to say, my trusting Pollyanna, rose-colored glasses did me no favors during my divorce. Unfortunately, my children are the ones who paid for my naiveté.

When contemplating divorce, you owe it to yourself and your child(ren) to envision the worst-case scenario and ask yourself if you could live with it. No matter how amicable your divorce may sound at first, things can change. The person you thought you knew so well can transform into a completely different person when someone else enters his or her life. What if your soon-to-be ex-spouse becomes involved with someone who either dislikes your children or uses them as pawns for financial gain? What if this results in your spouse becoming MIA for the rest of their lives? Will you be financially equipped to meet the needs of your children as well as yourself if your spouse fails, "forgets," or refuses to make child support payments?

Please try everything under the sun to save your marriage, from marriage counseling to perhaps a second honeymoon (or third or fourth!).

STRANGER DANGER

And then there was the general public. Remember during pregnancy when you had to deal with unwanted belly touching and intrusive questions? Those folks who used to offer their sage advice and wisdom such as "Ohh, you're carrying your baby so high. It must be a girl!" will now make a comeback, oftentimes with unsolicited medical advice. "Did you say your daughter is seven months old? Do you mean weeks? Hmm, have you tried goat's milk?"

No matter how well intentioned these comments might be, they can be triggering and put you on the defensive. I found that having some prepared responses ready really helped me from becoming a full-on agoraphobe in those early days.

> *Remember, you are in control. It's up to you how much (if any!) information you want to share.*

In time, I learned when, how much, and with whom to share. If a total stranger at the grocery store asked, "Are you sure your baby is ten months old?" (after asking me how old she was), I would simply smile and say, "Yep, and she's the happiest ten-month-old I know!" as I turned in the other direction.

Conversely, it was very hurtful for me when Kathryn would be dressed adorably, and there would be zero comments. Not a single one. Since I was also the mom of Kathryn's older sister, Ann, I knew how effusive people can be when they see a cute baby. Learning to cope with radio silence became my new norm.

Remember, you are in control. It's up to you how much (if any!) information you want to share. If ever there was a time for boundaries, it's now! As Kathryn's occupational therapist once told me, "You can use these times as an opportunity to educate if you'd like, but you don't owe an explanation to anybody." As Kathryn got older, I actually welcomed questions from children in particular.

Once Kathryn's differences were clearly apparent, she seemed to become invisible in the eyes of most teens and adults. When children asked what was wrong with her, I would welcome their innocent questions. At a time in our society when we have countless ribbons, bracelets, and full months devoted to everything from breast cancer awareness to Lou Gehrig's disease, I consider these interactions as valuable opportunities for special needs awareness. These interactions would typically go something like this:

> "Thank you for asking! What is your name? Well, Brandon, this is my daughter Kathryn, and just like some people might be born with ear problems or eye problems, she was born with some problems in her brain. Her brain works differently than yours or mine, so she looks different too. We're all so different. It's just that Kathryn's differences are more noticeable than others. She has a lot in common with us too. She loves to laugh, eat cookies, and float in swimming pools! I sure appreciate you asking me about her!"

I'd like to think that these encounters left young people like Brandon feeling a little less uneasy when encountering people with disabilities. Of course, if your child is higher functioning and verbal, you wouldn't want to share information like this in their presence. The key point is to keep your interactions positive. Typically, whenever a child asked what was wrong with Kathryn, the parent would immediately swoop in and shush them, conveying that their child was being rude. I tried to counteract this by welcoming the child's question and providing a positive answer at their level.

For instance, instead of saying, "She can't walk," I'd say, "Her wheelchair really helps her get around!" Rather than focusing on what was "wrong" with her, I would communicate how Kathryn just had a different way of being.

GUILT IS NOT YOUR FRIEND

Guilt is a powerful emotion. You know how I said that time is on your side regarding grief? Conversely, time can work to deepen your sense of guilt rather than relieve it. If you hold on to guilt and ruminate over any perceived action you did or did not take in the past, it will only grow and seep into other areas of your life. Guilt is best left as an emotion, not as a lifestyle.

For many of us parents, guilt seems to be a common denominator among us. It typically begins with questioning if your child's disability was your fault and then grows from there. Each one of us

Guilt is best left as an emotion, not as a lifestyle.

has our own story. For those of you who have other children, you may feel guilty that they're being neglected or that you may not have the same loving feelings for your child with special needs that you have for your other child. You feel you're doing too much—or too little. You feel guilty when you feel sad or disappointed, and you feel guilty when you feel angry. You may even feel guilty for feeling guilty!

Please hear me out. What parent would feel joy and gratitude that their child has intellectual and developmental disabilities? Yes, down the road you will experience joy as well as many amazing life lessons. But the truth is, whatever the diagnosis, it's nothing to rejoice over. Again, in time, you will come to love your child so much that you won't even be able to imagine them any other way, but is this what your heart of hearts would have chosen? I've said it before, and I'll say it again: as a human, of course you're going to feel a wide range of emotions, and not all are going to be pretty. It is 100% understandable. Feeling guilty for your sadness or disappointment is understandable, but you have done nothing to feel guilty about.

In Kathryn's last days on earth, I felt so much love and acceptance for her that I felt tremendous gratitude that she was exactly the way she was, but those feelings did not come overnight. I was the Queen of Guilt in the early days because of the feelings Kathryn brought up for me. Quite frankly, when she was a baby, I felt embarrassed to go out in public with her. She would arch her neck and back in a way that rivaled the most skilled contortionist. And while other babies would soothe themselves with their "loveys" in the form of soft toys and treasured blankets, Kathryn found comfort in having a Tupperware colander over her face. Every single detail about her was different. My friend Randy, who is a family therapist, used to say, "If it's hysterical, it's historical." In other words, there is personal history behind every emotional "hysteria." I had history, all right.

Growing up, my parents were very different from my friends' parents and the parents I saw on TV in the 1960s, and it caused me to feel embarrassed during much of my childhood. It didn't help that both of my parents were a good 10 years older than my peers' parents as well. While I watched other fathers in their fine suits drive their new cars to their important jobs, my father would spend his days watching television in his recliner due to his heart condition, dressed in pajamas or leisure wear. My mother was the bare-faced woman wearing a kerchief on her head as she chopped wood outside while the other moms channeled their inner Carol Brady as they hosted swanky dinner parties in pretty new dresses. I felt like I was on the set of *Ma and Pa Kettle* when I longed to live with the family of

The Brady Bunch. As I got older, I felt tremendous guilt for feeling this way about my two very kind and loving parents.

We're all such complex creatures with our own unique histories. It's only human that some pretty deep emotions are going to be triggered by your child's condition. This is a time for self-compassion and healing, not misplaced guilt. Let me ask you this: When you were pregnant, did you do anything to intentionally harm your child? Have you ever done anything to harm your child? No? Then please know, once and for all, that you are not at fault for your child's condition. Your days of feeling guilty are over. Done. Finished.

A personal example of mine is that around three weeks before Kathryn's birth, I was sitting quietly at work when out of nowhere, Kathryn began moving like crazy in utero. I had never felt anything like it. It was like a kickboxing class in my womb, complete with jabs and roundhouse kicks. It lasted for maybe 30 seconds and then her movements went back to normal.

When Kathryn had her first seizure at age two, I thought back to that moment during my pregnancy. I wondered if perhaps Kathryn had a seizure in utero, but her doctor told me that unborn babies do not have seizures. It wasn't until recently that I googled "Do babies have seizures in the womb" and read this: "Some theories suggest that these movements are caused by the umbilical cord being wrapped around the baby, and subsequently the fetus makes movements to try to shake it off."[10]

Away I went down the rabbit hole of guilt and self-blame again. Why didn't I go straight to my doctor that day and demand an ultrasound? These are the mind games that we parents can play, and it's a perfect example of irrational guilt.

I can play Monday morning quarterback all I want, but it is absolutely useless to guess whether or not it would have caused a different outcome for Kathryn had I "demanded" an ultrasound on that day.

The fact is that by 37 weeks (when Kathryn was born), 37% of babies have the cord wrapped around their necks[11] anyway, so do you really think my ob-gyn would have rushed to schedule me for an ultrasound at 34 weeks? Babies are born every day with cords wrapped around their necks, and it can't be prevented. When considering all the facts vs. my irrational guilt, I chose to let it go and know that Kathryn's medical team and I did the best we could all those years ago.

As humans, we will feel guilt for some of our actions. We may even deserve it because who doesn't mess up from time to time?! That's called having a healthy conscience. Ideally, though, guilt should motivate you to make your "wrongs" right again. Period. Here are some tips for processing *this* kind of guilt:

- Identify what you're feeling guilty about.

- Ask yourself if you can fix the situation by being accountable for it and then take the steps to make things right. In other words, acknowledge that you messed up. Use your words to apologize and seek to remedy any past mistake(s). Some situations might be beyond your control, but you can still take responsibility and acknowledge your role in whatever happened.

- Don't beat yourself up. Treat yourself with the kindness and compassion you would extend to a friend. Let the past stay in the past and learn from the event rather than ruminating over it.

- And whatever you do, beware of misplaced, irrational, or toxic guilt.[12] No one should have the power to place any guilt on you, and never feel guilty for simply having healthy boundaries. So you said no to working at your daughter's school bake sale? No guilt necessary, my friend. You've got enough on your plate.

Still feeling guilt? You may find it helpful to talk with a mental health professional about this issue. Please don't let these feelings linger.

TEASING AND BULLYING

One benefit of Kathryn being so profoundly disabled was that she was never teased or bullied in school. Even if she were, she wouldn't recognize it or care. Nevertheless, children do tend to tease each other, and this can be especially hurtful for children with special needs. All children deserve to thrive in an environment free from bullying. Ways that you can help your child are:

- When your child tells you she is being bullied, listen carefully and validate her feelings by paraphrasing what she says and by empathizing what she must be feeling: "So Caitlin said you couldn't play with her and the other girls because you are 'stupid'? I can totally understand how that must have hurt your feelings."

- Help build their confidence: "You are so smart to tell me about this." Also praise your child for her areas of strength: "One of the things I love so much about you is that you would never talk that way to anyone because you are so thoughtful and kind."

- Communicate with your child's teacher about the incident. Ideally, before incidents of bullying even occur, it is helpful to ask if the school staff and students receive training in bullying. It's always best to address bullying before it even takes place. Some schools have adopted a buddy system for children with special needs, and you may want to explore this idea with your child's teacher.

For more ideas, a great resource is StopBullying.gov.

When any child is bullied because of his or her disability and it creates a hostile environment at school, it may be considered "disability harassment." Under Section 504 of the Rehabilitation Act of 1973 and Title II of the Americans with Disabilities Act of 1990, the school must address the harassment.

YOUR SELF-WORTH

Lastly, even your very self-worth will be challenged. You may cease thinking about your own appearance and your prior interests. Politics, health, career, working out, socializing, hobbies all get put on the back burner as you obsess over your child's well-being. This is why I wrote Chapter Ten, "A Time for Joy and Perpetual Self-Care." You have somehow got to hold on to your own sense of self. That woman or man you were before you began this journey is still there. Please pay attention to your feelings and use them as a signal for what you need to do. This is not selfishness. Rather, it is survival. And when all else fails, remember the words of Mark Twain: "When you can't get a compliment any other way, pay yourself one."

CHAPTER NINE

DEFINING MOMENTS AS KATHRYN'S MOTHER

What seems to us as bitter trials
are often blessings in disguise.
– Oscar Wilde

Throughout Kathryn's life, I experienced certain defining moments. Each one of them left me with that kind of Aha! awareness that invariably led me to some form of transformation. You undoubtedly will experience these as well, but here are a few of mine, along with the lessons I learned from them. My hope is that you may learn from some of them too.

KATHRYN AND I EACH HAD OUR OWN SEPARATE JOURNEYS

One time when a friend told me about an interesting choice her grown daughter made, she said, "Oh well; it's *her* story!" Those words flipped a switch within me. It reminded me of when Kathryn was a baby, and I was going through a dark-night-of-the-soul period. I wondered if I would ever get over the grief, but Kathryn's father pointed out that I was not disabled. Without underestimating the role of parenthood, he reminded me that I still had my own life—separate from our daughter's.

> *As simplistic as it sounds, knowing that I did not have to stop living because of my daughter's diagnosis was an epiphany for me.*

When our babies depend upon us for their very survival, the thought of them as separate entities is so difficult to grasp. You may even have visions of them growing up to be little extensions of yourself. Who hasn't at one time or another felt that ego-driven delight when your child appears to be a "chip off the old block"? The truth remains that each child comes into the world the author of his or her own story, separate from us.

Just because I grieved over my daughter's inability to coordinate her arms and legs didn't mean I couldn't rejoice in my own ability to run, dance, or reign supreme on the tennis court. As simplistic as it sounds, knowing that I did not have to stop living because of my daughter's diagnosis was an epiphany for me. And so I decided to "put my oxygen mask on first," and help both my daughters *and myself* be all we could be. As the author Dodinsky once said, "Be there for others, but never leave yourself behind."[13]

SOMETIMES ALL YOU NEED IS A GOOD CRY!

When Kathryn was around 18 months old, I ran out to Krogers for a few groceries while my girls' father stayed home with them. In the checkout line, who should be standing next to me but a woman from my Lamaze class. I remembered her well because she planned to name her daughter Catherine, so we bonded in class over that. She instantly recognized me and excitedly introduced me to her daughter who greeted me with a big smile and actual spoken words. The mom remembered that I was naming my daughter Kathryn, so as she was lamenting how she could barely keep up with her daughter these days, she laughed and said, "I'm sure your Kathryn is running all over the place too!"

In that moment, I wanted the floor to open up and swallow me whole. Instead, I simply told her there had been some complications at birth. I no longer remember if I even bought what was in my cart. All I remember was wishing her well and quickly returning home. I couldn't get to my bedroom fast enough, but first, it felt really important to me to be an example to my daughter Ann. I calmly told her what transpired at the store and shared that it had made me feel very sad. I told her that I just needed to cry for a little bit and how important it is for us to express our emotions when we feel sad and that it's just a natural part of life.

Prior to this day, I think my emotions had been so stuck that I hadn't been able to cry. In retrospect, I don't think I had cried in over 10 years, since the death of my beloved father. A few of Kathryn's health care professionals had even given me a list of sad movies for me to watch, hoping it would prime the pump, so to speak. These were people who understood the importance of expressing grief rather than bottling it up.

As painful as it was, that day was a turning point for me, and I haven't had any difficulty crying ever since! Kathryn's health care professionals definitely were on to something in their insistence that I somehow break my emotional dam.

Scientific literature abounds on the mood-enhancing and stress-relieving effects of crying. Research indicates that crying elevates our levels of endorphins and oxytocin (known as "feel good" hormones) and helps us to return to our baseline or even above where we were.[14] Conversely, if we do not release all the emotional energy we're feeling, we are prone to distract ourselves with anything from binging on Netflix to overeating or misusing alcohol or drugs.

I think some of us would be more emotionally healthy if we embraced this quote from an unknown author: "Crying is not a sign of weakness; it's a courageous expression of emotions that leads to strength."

BITTER TRIALS ARE OFTEN BLESSINGS IN DISGUISE

When Kathryn was around three years old, I had a life-changing dream. I share it here because I feel that it can pertain to you as well.

The dream began with everyone around me preparing to drive from San Diego to Bellingham, Washington. I watched as people waved to each other as they got in their big, comfortable cars.

Beside me was a tiny, paint-chipped tricycle. Someone cheerfully told me that it was what *I* would be driving to Bellingham. As the other cars sped off down the freeway, I stood there in disbelief. How could I go anywhere on a tricycle? I was angry, confused—and all alone. Surely it was a mistake and someone would soon be bringing me a car too. A tricycle simply wouldn't work for me. Tricycles are too small, they're slow, and—well, people stare at adults riding tricycles. All of which I found to be true—at first. But after a while I noticed that all that pedal pumping was creating some nice muscles in my legs, and the brisk air against my face did feel kind of good. I began to smile and before long, children and a few knowing adults began to smile back at me from their cars.

After a while, the cars could only be heard in the distance. My little tricycle and I were on a beautiful path reserved just for bicycles. What joy I felt when I spotted some exquisite wildflowers beneath my feet and a beautiful stream on my right! I looked off in the distance at the speeding cars and felt fortunate to be experiencing these hidden treasures.

Pretty soon 10-year-old Ann pulled up alongside me, she too on a tricycle. She seemed right at home in our new environment. She was glad we could experience this unexpected joy together.

"Ann!" I shouted. "The sign says it's only 41 miles to Bellingham!" I had been enjoying my journey so much that I hadn't even been thinking of Bellingham or of the other cars which were no longer visible to me. At that point I woke up.

I felt like a different person after that dream. Whenever I had my moments of thinking about what might have been,

I thought of wildflowers and strong legs and a quiet little path and hidden treasures, and I knew that everything was exactly the way it was supposed to be on my unplanned parenting journey.

THINKING BEYOND MY OWN LIFE FOR KATHRYN

A very powerful turning point was when I taught a Sunday school class for adults with special needs. These folks mainly had Down syndrome and mild-to-moderate intellectual disabilities. Each of the students lived happily with their parents. Over time, though, I witnessed the devastation that took place when these adults needed to be placed elsewhere when their parents were either no longer able to care for them or had passed away. It was then that I decided it would be best to make this adjustment for Kathryn while I was still alive and could help with the transition. Author Pearl Buck made this decision when her daughter was nine. In her book, *The Child Who Never Grew*, she wrote, "We have to think beyond our own lives for them."[15] I wasn't sure of the timing at that point, but I knew that this was in our future.

Just as I needed a tribe, I knew that one day Kathryn would need her own. Years later, I was reminded of this whenever I visited her in her group home. She loved our car rides together, but she was always just as thrilled to return to her people. She would push me away to go sit in "her chair" in the family room with the others. They were all much higher functioning than Kathryn and enjoyed watching game shows. Although Kathryn didn't understand any of it, she seemed so happy and content to just sit with them in the late afternoons each day.

IT'S OKAY TO ADMIT YOUR LIMITATIONS

Perhaps one of the most pivotal moments for me was when Kathryn was around 15, and her group home was being evacuated due to a local wildfire. This meant that Kathryn was going to spend the night with me. At this time in her development, she was going through a phase where she had to wear overalls and bodysuits at all times because of her strong propensity for fecal smearing and ingestion, a behavior not uncommon for children with autism. Changing her diapers was especially challenging because she was very strong and very determined to gain access to the contents in her diaper. Even when using all my strength, our diaper-changing sessions ended up with feces spread on the wall, underneath her fingernails, and on my clothes. This situation eventually culminated with me lying next to her (after cleaning up, of course), in tears, and telling her I was sorry that I was not able to take care of her. As a parent, to admit that you are neither physically nor emotionally capable of caring for your child is a sobering and humbling realization.

Again, this is where perspective comes in. I could care for my daughter in my own way. I may not have been able to change her diapers, but I could still advocate for her in the medical and educational communities, and I could still care for her by attending to her interests, such as taking her out for car rides.

I may have failed at changing diapers, but that didn't make me a failure as her parent. This limitation did not define me as a parent. I knew that I would always be her #1 advocate, and that nothing could ever diminish my love for her.

Several years after this, Kathryn's sister Ann and I struggled to change Kathryn's diaper while standing up in a bathroom stall while she was in a prom dress. Ann and I had been thrilled when we found out that a prom was being hosted for teenagers with special needs, complete with limos and disco balls! We were so in hopes that Kathryn might enjoy all the lights and music. We couldn't have been more wrong! It was all a fiasco, culminating with our bathroom stall debacle. The prom committee had thought of everything except for areas to change students who needed that service. Neither Ann nor I was very proficient at changing Kathryn's diapers in the best of situations, but standing up in a bathroom stall with Kathryn in a formal prom dress? This was the disaster of all disasters, but it ended with both of us huddled together on the lavatory floor absolutely belly laughing over what diaper changing losers we were. I guess you could say it was one of those bonding moments we'll never forget. To this day, we are in awe of how skillful Kathryn's caregivers were. We left shortly after this, and Kathryn couldn't have been happier to return to the safe haven of her home!

> *I may have failed at changing diapers, but that didn't make me a failure as her parent.*

CHAPTER TEN

A TIME FOR JOY AND PERPETUAL SELF-CARE!

If you want to find inner happiness, go outside on a nice day with lots of sun and blue sky. Even if you stand at a window and look out over the city at the cloudless sky, like we're doing now, you'll eventually find happiness.
— ANNE FRANK

Experiencing joy depends a lot upon how we choose to perceive any given situation we're in. When I was in the thick of my sad days when Kathryn was very young, I discovered that she liked being held outside on our patio swing chair. During one of these times, I suddenly and unexpectedly felt my old friend "joy" begin to stir within me. The sky that day was quintessential East County San Diego, bright blue with lots of sunshine. It made me think of what Anne Frank wrote about finding happiness by simply looking at the blue sky. I told myself that if she could experience happiness while hiding from the Third Reich in a cramped attic, I could experience it too. This stirring of joy within me felt good, so I decided to make a point of looking for it in every way I could.

I discovered that the better care I took of myself, the more joy I felt, so I learned to prioritize self-care. Everybody's talking about self-care these days to the point where it sometimes feels like, "Enough, already!" Right? Not to sound overly dramatic, but you really can only neglect self-care for so long before anxiety, anger, depression, insomnia, and social isolation begin to kick in. In time, this can lead to a total sense of hopelessness as well as chronic illness. Never in your life have you needed to cultivate your mental and physical health more, and the fact is that self-care goes a long way in helping you feel a greater sense of well-being and hope.

GET YOUR ZZZS

Self-care is about so much more than manis, pedis, and aromatherapy candles. The quality of our sleep and diet tops the list in importance when it comes to our overall well-being. You cannot function without these two.

According to the National Sleep Foundation, adults between ages 18 and 64 should aim for seven to nine hours of sleep per night.[16] A lack of sleep on a regular basis affects not only your immune system, but your ability to cope with stress and your overall mood as well. Research has shown that the odds for recovering from depression are against you when you get fewer than seven hours of sleep per night.[17] Chances are you already know all the natural remedies such as taking a warm bath at bedtime, drinking soothing teas like chamomile, and avoiding caffeine after noon, so I'm not going to belabor that. What I will say is that when you prioritize getting enough sleep, your mental health will be given a leg up. In Kathryn's early days, I learned firsthand that a lack of sleep affected my well-being more than anything else. I couldn't agree more with the inventor E. Joseph Cossman who once said, "The best bridge between despair and hope is a good night's sleep."

YOU ARE WHAT YOU EAT!

Next to sleep, I'm a wreck whenever I don't limit my intake of sugar and processed foods. According to researchers in the journal *The Lancet Psychiatry*, "Diet is as important to psychiatry as it is to cardiology, endocrinology, and gastroenterology."[18] Foods specifically shown to improve your mental health are those that are packed with vitamins, minerals, antioxidants, and amino acids. Foods found in the Mediterranean diet are good examples, such as fresh vegetables, legumes, whole grains, fish, eggs, and healthy fats, especially olive oil. Conversely, studies have linked the Western diet to a greater risk of depression.[19] The Western diet typically includes foods such as takeout or fast food, red meat, high-sugar desserts and other refined carbs and processed foods. The bottom line is to focus on whole foods and healthy oils like olive, avocado, and coconut. Taking the time each day to prepare healthy meals makes all the difference in how you feel.

TO THINE OWN SELF BE TRUE!

Another important component of self-care for me was being true to myself. While some women really benefited from their church's women's retreats or specific support groups, those activities just weren't for me. I tried them, but they all left me feeling more depleted than inspired.

A dear friend shared an analogy with me that greatly helped me concerning this. Since we both grew up in the Pacific Northwest, she brought up the unique needs of rhododendrons. These flowering bushes were beyond plentiful in Gig Harbor, Washington, back in the day. You didn't need to care for them in any way; they simply thrived on their own. But what if you moved to Tucson, Arizona, and replanted them there? It wouldn't take long for them to simply wither and die. Sometimes we forget that we are as unique as the plants we see in nature. Each one of us has unique needs in which we can flourish and thrive.

It's important to ask yourself what your soul needs at this time in your life.

While some may find support groups and women's retreats a lifeline, those environments may be kryptonite to others. It's important to ask yourself what your soul needs at this time in your life. What inspired me was taking classes in subjects that interested me, meeting dear friends for quality one-on-one time, and going on solo hikes in the sunshine. What inspires you? You owe it to yourself and others to listen to your true self and to seek out the environments and experiences that enable you to be your best self.

GET MOVING!

Getting enough exercise did wonders for my physical and mental health. Going to the gym every day helped me to get plenty of oxygenated blood pumping into my brain. Not only did that help me stay mentally sharp, but it also produced endorphins that are known to cause feelings of euphoria and well-being. Being in shape did wonders for my self-confidence too, which had really taken a beating in Kathryn's early days.

Find some form of exercise you enjoy. Whether you go for daily nature walks, do kickboxing, go for a swim, or sign up for Zumba, it's all good if it gets you up and moving.

DON'T NEGLECT YOUR OWN MEDICAL HEALTH

Along with all of the above, make sure you schedule your annual physical/blood labs, mammograms, and dental care. Just as you would never skip one of your child's medical appointments, you'll want to be just as diligent with your own.

SEEK OUT JOY EVERY DAY

As you commit yourself to these basic self-care tips, you will be on your way to being the best version of yourself. Not only will you feel more focused, happier, and calm, but you'll be able to help your child better as well. It's true that you can't pour from an empty cup, but when you prioritize self-care, your cup may never be empty.

Ask yourself what makes your heart sing. Whatever it is, if it makes you feel alive, it is not an indulgence. Rather, it is a necessity in your life and will help you handle stress. Check out respite services in your area and schedule time for yourself to:

> *Ask yourself what makes your heart sing.*

- Spend some time in nature.

- Find some form of movement you LOVE: martial arts, yoga, fencing, tap dancing, tennis.

- Soak in a luxuriously scented bubble bath, complete with candles and a glass of wine or other favorite beverage.

- Have a regular date night with your significant other or simply a friend.

- Get a massage or facial!

- Go window shopping.

- Take a class just for fun, be it pottery, stained glass art, or learning French.

- Go to the library or your favorite bookstore and select a book just for fun.

- Find joy EVERY day!

CHAPTER ELEVEN

PRACTICAL TIPS FROM ONE PARENT TO ANOTHER

*Life truly begins only after you have
put your house in order.*
— MARIE KONDO

ORGANIZATIONAL TIPS

Declutter your life! Clutter leads to stress. You already have enough stress, so why not reduce some of the stress you can control by creating a peaceful environment in your home. Room by room, get rid of anything that does not serve a necessary function or bring you joy. And while you're at it, it's time to delete your 12,743 emails that go back to 2005. If you haven't read them by now, you can probably survive just fine without them. It's amazing how liberating it can feel when you've cleared all the out-of-control messes in your home, car, purses, and technology of choice.

Take notes. My constant companion during Kathryn's young childhood was a notebook I always kept with me. In it, I would take notes at her doctor's appointments as well as daily observations such as this one from April 17, 1992:

> "I made two attempts to take Kathryn outside—one in her sling and one in her stroller. Both attempts were disastrous due to her hypersensitivity to sunlight. She cried nonstop until I got her back in the house. Her distress seemed to trigger CP posturing. This was at 9 a.m., and the sun wasn't even that bright. Conversely, why does she love bright indoor lighting so much?"

It was really helpful to have everything written down in one place that I could refer to when needed. Sometimes in the middle of the night I would jot down questions or little reminders that would pop into my head. Sure, there are apps for this, but if you're like me, you'll find that there's nothing like a simple paper notebook.

Using the Notes app on my phone, I kept a "Kathryn" document where I stored all the information I needed at her many appointments. This included all her numbers from her Medical ID number to her California ID, as well as phone numbers and addresses for all six of her doctors, pharmacy, day program, and social worker. On this document, I had all of her meds listed along with the dosages, and even a record of all her seizures and hospital stays. I can't begin to tell you what an invaluable resource this was.

For her IEPs, IPPs (Individualized Program Plan), and medical records, I used an old-school filing system at home with labeled file folders for each year.

When Kathryn attended school and then later her day program, a school-home notebook was used for communication. This consisted of a spiral notebook in her backpack that traveled back and forth between school and her group home. In it, her teacher wrote down any observations, concerns, or questions she had, and her care provider in turn would communicate any questions she had as well as to communicate upcoming doctor's appointments that would necessitate her missing school, etc.

TIME MANAGEMENT

Take an honest inventory of how you use your time. It's time to let go of everything (and perhaps everyone?) who depletes you. Sometimes we hold on to old habits and activities like we hold on to old clothes. They may have served you splendidly at one time, but how do they contribute to you on your journey today?

It's time to let go of everything (and perhaps everyone?) who depletes you.

As you schedule your days, be sure to schedule daily recuperation time. Yes, I said recuperation! When I used to do mini marathons, I would always make sure I had nothing on my calendar for the rest of the day. I learned from experience that if I didn't listen to the needs of my body, there would be hell to pay later! What my body needed after these marathons was down time in the form of a nap and then taking it easy at home. When you raise a child with special needs, it can often feel like a series of mini marathons. Listen to the needs of your body, mind, and spirit. Schedule time just to take it easy for a little bit.

HELPING YOUR CHILD WITH BASIC LIFE SKILLS

We all take care of ourselves each day by washing our hands, brushing our teeth, brushing our hair, etc. Having regular times each day for these habits helps to instill a comforting routine.[20] No matter what level your child is at, they will come to recognize a certain rhythm to their days when these habits are consistently done at the same time. Before meals and after using the bathroom, we wash our hands, every morning after breakfast we brush our teeth, and we brush them again at bedtime. A bathing and shampooing routine should be established too. If you have other children at home, it is great to enlist their help with some of these habits, such as brushing their teeth together.

Depending upon your child's abilities, they can also be assigned a household chore. Kathryn's "chore" was picking up the mail. Of course she had to be assisted in everything from walking to the mailbox to opening it up, being handed the mail, and then helping her to close the box, but it is routines like these that go a long way in making your child feel like they're a contributing member in your family.

DRESSING YOUR CHILD

Prior to Kathryn's arrival in my life, I could not understand why parents of special needs kids didn't dress their children better. Oh, how I learned to regret some of my ill-informed judgments in those days, as in, "Why would they dress their son in *that*?" or "They could at least comb their daughter's hair!" It didn't take long before I fully understood some of the challenges parents face when dressing their child and sending them off to school. We didn't have "adaptive clothing" back in the day, so we parents made our own adaptations as well as we could. For example, despite Kathryn not having clothing sensitivities, she went through a phase in her early teen years when we couldn't keep a shirt on her. As you can imagine, whenever we were in public, I couldn't turn my back on her for a minute! Coupled with this was her propensity for getting into her diapers. It also didn't help that Kathryn's head was rarely still. Because of her head constantly turning back and forth in her wheelchair, in the car, and on her bed, she had bald patches, and the rest of her naturally beautiful hair was always matted. All of these issues meant her care provider and I had to come up with all kinds of ways to modify her wardrobe. For most of her life, Kathryn had to wear footed onesie pajamas backwards at night, along with a belt cinched at her waist. And during a period in time when bodysuits were nearly impossible to find, Kathryn's care provider would make them for her. Was I ever humbled by my earlier judgments of parents' wardrobe choices!

Today, when you do a Google search for "adaptive clothing for children with disabilities," you will discover all kinds of solutions for so many issues parents experience. I have the greatest respect for moms like Nikki Puzzo who designed a pair of pants for her five-year-old daughter with cerebral palsy. These pants could be put on over her leg casts after she had an operation. When the little girl's doctors saw her wearing them at a post-op appointment, they encouraged Nikki to make more. And so, Nikki, along with her friend and fellow mom Joanne DiCamillo, founded be-free, LLC. Their mission is "to offer a product that provides freedom during a time when freedom feels so far away."[21] It is absolutely heartwarming to think of how these women have helped so many people around the world to feel comfortable and even stylish!

Whatever dressing issue you may face, seek out a solution from your doctor, online community of parents, or simply do a Google search. If all else fails, let Nikki and Joanne inspire you to develop your own adaptive clothing line!

CHAPTER TWELVE

IT'S VACATION TIME!

When all else fails, take a vacation.
– BETTY WILLIAMS

You may not be able to travel like you once did, but you do not need to rule it out entirely. Travel can still be a very enjoyable experience with enough careful planning.

Wherever your vacation destination takes you, you'll want to make sure you bring all your basics such as sunscreen, bug spray, medications, and all your medical info and contacts, as well as any beloved comforts of home such as favorite toys and "loveys." So many children with disabilities thrive on routine, so any way you can incorporate that into your travels is ideal in the form of mealtimes, bedtimes, etc.

Before embarking on a week-long journey to the beach or theme park, you may want to test the waters by just going on an overnight trip where you spend the night in a hotel or another family member's house. Depending upon your child's abilities, you could show them photos of where you are going and talk with them about any fears or questions they may have.

Once you're at your destination, always plan for some quiet time alone with your child. This could be heading back to your hotel room for a little bit of R&R when you're out at a theme park, or simply retreating to an empty room together while at a family member's house.

THEME PARKS

With all theme parks, you'll want to do your research ahead of time. Find out where their medical office is located as well as their nursery and a place to change diapers for an older child. Of course you will want to avoid going during weeks like spring break, the peak of summer, or the week before and after Christmas.

Depending upon your child's needs, you may want to buy noise-canceling headphones for your child to wear, and if your child is very sensitive to bright lights, sunglasses may be in order. Whenever I took Kathryn to theme parks, I would pack snacks for her, and I wouldn't dream of taking her without her favorite "lovey"; first, this was a Tupperware colander, and then beginning at age nine, it was her Mozart Magic Cube.

DISNEYLAND

Disneyland has it down pat when it comes to serving the needs of guests with disabilities! The Disneyland Resort offers a host of services to help guests with cognitive disabilities—including those on the autism spectrum, such as:

- Advance ticket purchase
- Stroller and wheelchair rental
- Strollers as wheelchairs
- Rider switch
- Accessing attractions
- Break areas
- Companion restrooms
- Attraction guides
- Dietary accommodations

They highly recommend that you purchase your park tickets for Disneyland Park and Disney California Adventure Park, including Magic Keys, in advance online at www.disneyland.com or by calling (714) 781-4636. To enter any of the theme parks, guests ages three and older will need a valid ticket and a theme park reservation.

An amazing resource is their "Attraction Details for Guests with Cognitive Disabilities." You can download this from the Disneyland website. It provides you with a detailed graph of every attraction at the park along with every detail you need to help you decide if the ride or attraction would be a good fit for your child. For example, it informs you of scents/smells, lighting effects, loud noises, periods of darkness, bumpiness, speed, whether or not the ride lifts from the ground, if it's wet, if there is an element of surprise, the type of restraint used, and the trip time. You may wish to print the graph if you'd prefer to have a hard copy.

Another indispensable resource you can download from their site is a 15-page resource guide for guests with cognitive disabilities including autism spectrum disorder (ASD). It will provide you with everything you need to know about planning your visit, like their "Rider Switch" service which enables you to experience whatever ride you want to go on while someone else from your party waits with your child who will not be riding. You then "swap" to enable the other party to enjoy the ride without having to wait in line again. This guide really leaves no stone unturned and will provide you with information about their Disability Access Service, DAS Advance, Genie, and Genie+ for your child who isn't able to tolerate extended waits in line.

You can also call their Disability Services at (407) 560-2547 or you can email them at disability.services@disneyland.com if you can't find the information you need within their resource guides.

The Walt Disney World Resort offers similar resources. I encourage you to visit any theme park's website to learn more about the services they provide for children with special needs.

Each one seems to have its own unique specialty, such as SeaWorld in Orlando that has partnered with The International Board of Credentialing and Continuing Education Standards (IBCCES), a global leader in online training and certification programs, to become designated as a Certified Autism Center™ (CAC). They are committed to offering specialized services to guests with autism and other special needs.

LEGOLAND® offers an Assisted Access Pass for guests with special needs, including autism, which allows them no wait time for the first ride, and then a reservation-like system for all subsequent rides.

AIR TRAVEL

Traveling by car is usually the first choice for parents with a child with special needs. Sometimes, though, it just makes more sense to fly. Traveling by plane does have it challenges, but hopefully the tips below will make your trip go smoothly. I am continually pleasantly surprised by how airports are accommodating the needs of the IDD community. Yesterday when I was at Newark Liberty International Airport, I was so impressed with their beautiful Sensory Room. It is an interactive space to help travelers who are "neurodivergent" and may become overwhelmed by a bustling and unfamiliar place. These spaces that are designed for those with autism, dementia, or other sensory-processing challenges or disabilities are now popping up in airports all across the nation, such as in Seattle, Pittsburgh, Miami, Phoenix, and Houston.

When traveling by air, every traveler, regardless of disability, must undergo security screening. As a former TSA officer and passenger support specialist, I screened a wide range of children with disabilities. TSA has a wonderful program called "TSA Cares." It is set up to assist travelers with disabilities and medical conditions. If you would like to schedule assistance at your airport's security checkpoint or if you have any questions whatsoever, do not hesitate to call them 72 hours prior to traveling. Their number is (855) 787-2227, and they are available Monday through Friday from 8:00 a.m. to 11:00 p.m. ET, and from 9:00 a.m. to 8:00 p.m. ET on weekends and holidays.

Most TSA checkpoints have at least one passenger support specialist that you can request, but even if they don't, they will provide you with a caring individual who will be happy to assist you. There are different screening requirements for children over 12, but they will explain that to you.

For the best security experience, you'll want to arrive at least several hours before your boarding time. Even if your child does not use a wheelchair, you may use the wheelchair line. If you have not already made prior arrangements through TSA Cares, you will inform the TSA officer who requests your ID that your child has a disability and that you would like assistance.

Children do not need to be removed from their wheelchairs, but the wheelchair itself will need to undergo screening. Similarly, if your child needs to be carried, you will be allowed to carry him or her. TSA officers are trained in screening whatever special needs you or your children have.

If you require special foods or liquids that are larger than the standard 3.4 ounces allowed on planes, this is also not a problem. You will need to remove them from your carry-on bag and inform the TSA officer that they are medically necessary. TSA will test each of these items so you will be able to travel with them. If you are traveling with an ice pack, be sure that it is in a frozen or partially frozen state. Along with this, you will want to inform the TSA officer of any special medical equipment you are traveling with such as IV bags, pumps, and syringes. You will want to take into consideration that if a medically necessary liquid, gel, or aerosol alarms during the screening process, it may require additional screening and may not be allowed. You can express any concerns you may have regarding this during your conversation with TSA Cares prior to your trip. If you do not want your medications to be screened by X-ray, you will need to inform a TSA officer. They will need to take additional steps to clear the item, and you will undergo additional screening procedures yourself, such as a full pat down and a more thorough screening of the rest of your property.

Of all the passengers with disabilities that I screened while working for TSA, I will always remember one family who brought their son with autism to the airport a few days prior to their travels. The boy presented me with a booklet he made with all the details concerning screening and what he could expect on their big day. His parents did an amazing job acknowledging and assisting him with the anxiety he was experiencing. You can only imagine how helpful it was for this boy to actually meet a TSA officer who praised him for his thoroughness and confirmed with him what he could expect. When their travel day arrived, this family sailed through the checkpoint because they were so well prepared, and I'll never forget the look of relief and joy on that boy's face!

Whether you're traveling with a child who is visually impaired, has a service animal, or is having a complete meltdown, TSA will work with you in using the appropriate screening method.

Now that you're through security and at your gate, you can let the gate agent know that your child requires early boarding. When the agent announces early boarding, you'll want to be in the gate area, ready to board first.

LODGING

Again, do your research. You know your child best. Might he love being in a swimming pool? Staying at a hotel with a pool might offer you the perfect opportunity to find out! If your child is very sensitive to changes, you may want to pack his own pillow and blanket for him.

STAYING WITH FAMILY

The success of staying with one of your family members requires preparation on both sides. You'll want to provide enough information to your family member so they can prepare for your arrival. Of course this depends upon how much time your family members have spent with your child, but you'll want to share the basics. If your son Jason has autism, you may want to remind them that he is very uncomfortable with hugs and kisses. It would be good to communicate to them how Jason thrives with routine so that you would like to try to maintain all your daily routines while staying with them. You may want to provide them with a list of foods your child loves as well as dislikes, and offer to bring some of his favorite foods with you!

With your child, it's a great idea to show them pictures of the family members' house as well as each of its members.

Depending upon your child's abilities, you might try doing Facetime with the family. They could show him where he will eat and sleep, and even the bathroom he will be using.

Enlist your child's input on what to pack, i.e., would he like to take some coloring books and crayons? A special toy, book, or pillow?

PREPARE A TRAVEL MELTDOWN KIT

I actually had these for both daughters when they were young. Of course, they contained different items. You will want to tailor it for your child. I didn't limit them to travel either. Kits like these come in handy while waiting at the doctor's office, in a long line at the grocery store, and countless other scenarios.

In a cosmetics bag, Ziploc bag, or even a large pencil case, try to always have some special distracters on hand. A few ideas include:

- A bottle of bubbles with a wand
- Small fidget toys (Amazon has a huge selection)
- A Slinky
- Silly Putty or Play Dough
- A tiny stuffed animal
- Stickers and a notepad
- A book
- Finger puppets
- A kaleidoscope
- A stress ball

CHAPTER THIRTEEN

PLANNING FOR THE FUTURE

*Let our advance worrying become
advance thinking and planning.*
– WINSTON CHURCHILL

Regardless of our child's abilities, as parents we all want to prepare our children for a happy and fulfilling future. As parents of a child with special needs, we simply have additional considerations and areas of focus.

CONSERVATORSHIP/GUARDIANSHIP

When your child turns 18, if he does not have the intellectual ability to understand his rights as an adult, you as the parent may want to be appointed as their conservator or legal guardian, unless you wish for an entity such as the Department of Developmental Services to make all decisions on your child's behalf. Each state may have its own wording on this, but in the state of California, I filed a petition with the court to become Kathryn's limited conservator. It was a very lengthy and involved process. A court investigator was assigned to the case, and I went to a hearing on Kathryn's behalf. It was a happy day when the judge appointed me as Kathryn's limited conservator. This enabled me to continue to have the final say on all medical, educational, and life decisions concerning her welfare.

Again, all of this varies by state, and not every child with disabilities will need a legal guardian when they reach legal age. Depending upon their ability to understand the information provided by professionals and ability to make sound decisions concerning their own care and safety, it may not be necessary.

WILLS AND TRUSTS

If you wish to leave an inheritance to your child, you will need to get legal advice regarding what type of will or trust is appropriate in your case.

Because Kathryn resided in a group home that was funded by MediCal (government funding in California), my attorney had me specify in my Last Will and Testament that she would be excluded from any of my assets. While as a parent, this felt painful to see in writing, it made sense in our situation. Had I not done this, any financial resources I left for her would have gone to the State of California rather than to her.

There are so many variables here that it is imperative you consult legal advice in your state. For example, in some cases, even a small life insurance policy left to your child could put her in a position of becoming disqualified for governmental funding.

Prior to meeting with an attorney, you will save yourself time and money if you thoroughly think through all your wishes. Prepare like crazy! Come with all your information such as any governmental benefits that your child receives, all of your financial information such as your assets, income, etc.

Because Kathryn was in a group home where not only the care provider, her family, and a staff of caregivers knew her well, I always felt confident that if I died suddenly, Kathryn's needs would continue to be understood and addressed. In the case of parents who live with their nonverbal grown son with special needs, for instance, if they should pass away suddenly, how well equipped would the new guardian be? Would they know if Jake loves broccoli with cheese, likes to go swimming in a local pool every Saturday, and is terribly frightened of cats? Most estate-planning documents specify that the same standard of living your child received in your lifetime should be maintained. While that might sound completely fine, it truly is in your adult child's best interests to communicate your wishes as *specifically* as possible. This is where an estate-planning file or notebook comes in handy. This is like a manual that describes every detail about your adult child from their every like and dislike to all their day-to-day routines and even how holidays are celebrated.

A word to the wise regarding selecting your attorney. Use the same care that you did in selecting your child's physicians. Choose one that listens to you and really seems to understand and care about you and your child's needs.

It is very helpful to get a referral from friends, family, or another parent of a child with special needs.

Explore all options. You may have free legal clinics in your area, and you can also research attorneys who will handle certain cases pro bono or at a reduced rate.

PRE-PAID FUNERAL PLANNING

When Kathryn was around 18 years old, her care provider suggested that I might want to take care of funeral planning at that time vs. later. As much as I didn't want to think about needing funeral care for Kathryn, I listened to the care provider's reasoning. She experienced firsthand how difficult it is for parents not only to have to deal with their child dying, but to have to make all the funeral arrangements at that time as well. She suggested I call our social worker who could provide information regarding an insurance benefit through the state of California that covered funeral care 100% when paid in advance.

Sadly, I did end up needing funeral care for Kathryn 13 years later, and I cannot stress enough how grateful I was that I had established a contact with a local funeral home ahead of time. After Kathryn was first diagnosed with terminal cancer, I called them, and within seconds, they had Kathryn's file in hand.

As the time drew nearer (ironically, Ann and I had scheduled an appointment with them the day before Kathryn passed), we sat down and revisited all the original services I had signed up for. Having an end-of-life plan in place meant that during the progression of Kathryn's cancer, I was able to fully focus on her without the added stress of locating a funeral home, planning the funeral, and paying for it.

Some prepaid plans enable you to lock in current costs, but ours did not. A lot had changed in 13 years, and I wish I had accounted for inflation back in 2010 when I first met with the funeral director. Thinking about Kathryn's funeral 13 years ago felt so abstract to me that I couldn't even wrap my head around it. Consequently, the details I chose back then were so different from what I wanted for her after her battle with breast cancer. Luckily, one of my daughter Ann's friends started a GoFundMe for us that covered the balance of our expenses, but if I could have gone back in time, I would have budgeted for more expenses, especially since this was so generously covered by the state of California. Finances aside, it felt comforting knowing that I already had a contact person and a place to go when the time came. I can't even imagine how stressful it would have been had I not taken care of this all those years ago.

The more details you can take care of now, the less stress it will create when you are going through one of the most emotional times of your life.

CHAPTER FOURTEEN

LESSONS I LEARNED FROM KATHRYN

While we try to teach our children all about life,
our children teach us what life is all about.
– Angela Schwindt

As I mentioned earlier, once I finished grieving over not having the perfect baby of my dreams, I got to work fixing her. I took Kathryn to OT and PT and I took classes through the Hadley School for the Blind and the Alexander Graham School for the Deaf. I went to seminars on gluten-free cooking and joined the Cerebral Palsy and Autism Societies. I spent days in university libraries researching what possibly went wrong and how I could fix it. It turned out that my "imperfect" daughter was pretty perfect after all. She began to be the ultimate teacher of my life, fixing me.

STRENGTH

I will forever be grateful for how Kathryn expanded my mind and heart. Because of Kathryn, I am stronger in every way. The best way to describe the strength I gained from her would be to share the following analogy with you.

If you saw a photo of my friend Jerene, you would be struck by her perfect athletic physique. You might think something along the lines of, "Must be nice!" or "I wonder what her secret is." She would be the first to tell you that there is no secret. A year prior to having her picture-perfect body, she hired a personal trainer and committed to following the regimen prescribed to her. For one solid year, she put in the work and never gave up. She ate healthful meals and worked out, never losing sight of her goal.

My daughter Kathryn was the personal trainer of my heart and soul. People sometimes ask me how I'm so happy. I can't help but think that it's because I went to the Kathryn Grady School of Life. And that is something I never could have visualized in those early days. I think Jerene probably had a better idea of her outcome than I did of mine. In those early days, I was too focused on my sadness, fear, and disappointment to think that anything positive could possibly come from my new life. Thankfully, I had the perfect personal trainer for me: Kathryn Grady. The program was pretty grueling at times, but I'm not sure I could have gotten the lasting results any other way.

As Glenn E. Manguarian says in the article, "Realizing What You're Made Of," those who have survived a traumatic, life-altering event sometimes emerge not just changed, but stronger and even more content than ever.[22] I have found this to be so true. He goes on to say that this isn't just "making the best of a bad situation." He describes how becoming permanently paralyzed after a disc rupture caused him to cut through the clutter to focus on what really matters. Through his adversity, he discovered the power of resilience. Parents of children with special needs witness and develop resilience in spades. When it comes to triumphing over adversities and setbacks, it's typically our resilience that saves the day vs. "toughness." Many times, being "tough" means that you've put on armor that deflects emotion. In contrast, resilience doesn't deflect challenges; rather, it absorbs them, and we end up rebounding stronger than before. Resilience gives us the ability to create a new way of being. What new possibilities lie ahead for you? What new future will you create as you go forward with your life?

AUTHENTICITY

Kathryn's authenticity taught me much about boundaries. She couldn't have cared less what anyone thought of her. If she didn't want you in her space, without a word or even a single facial expression, she would take your hand and escort you to the door. No longer do I care so much what others think of me either, and I think that a lot of this was from Kathryn's influence.

My journey with Kathryn forced me to rethink my life, my goals, and beliefs. Along the way, I learned what truly mattered to me as well as what didn't. This turned out to be very liberating, as I no longer wanted to waste my time on irrelevant matters. My life became more focused on moving forward in an authentic way vs. clinging to the way I was before Kathryn entered the world.

UNCONDITIONAL LOVE

Most of all, I learned about unconditional love from Kathryn. Would I have loved her any more had she been able to talk or speak seven languages? No, I loved her exactly the way she was.

Kathryn never uttered a word or even made eye contact with me. She typically pushed me away when I arrived after traveling 10 hours to see her from my new home in Kentucky, but I LOVED her with all my heart. I still love her so much it hurts, and that is because she's my daughter, and THAT is how I perceive how God loves us. As his sons and daughters, we don't have to be perfect or even remotely close to perfect for him to love us.

SAY YES TO ALL THINGS GOOD FROM DIVERSITY TO ASSISTANCE

It's said that it takes a village to raise a child. When your child has special needs, it sometimes feels like it takes an entire county! Somewhere along the line, I learned that I didn't have to be on this journey alone. I got in the habit of saying, "Yes, thank you!" to every good thing that came our way.

Thirty-one years after Kathryn's birth, I stood at her Celebration of Life Service, and when I looked out at the room full of beloved people (Kathryn's "county"!), I realized that if it were not for her, I wouldn't have known a single soul in that room, except for family members. Because of your child, the most amazing people you have ever met are about to enter your life.

DON'T WORRY

Because of Kathryn, I have a new relationship with worry. I soon learned that worrying never helps or changes anything. I also learned not to sweat the small stuff, and when your child is intubated in the ICU while being strapped down on a hospital bed, everything else feels like small stuff.

Of course it's only natural to worry when initially faced with a tragedy. What I'm referring to, though, is being locked into worry, i.e., when it becomes a pattern and a way of being. There comes a time when you need to shift focus. For me, it started with the question of, "How can I best help Kathryn?"

All of these lessons have contributed to me liking the person I am today. I'm not sure if I would be so keen on the me who never attended the Kathryn Grady School of Life. Had I not gone on this unplanned journey, would I be as compassionate, as nonjudgmental, or as open minded?

From Kathryn's first year, I began learning the wisdom in just taking one day at a time, as mentioned in this excerpt from my journal when she was not quite one year old:

My Dear Daughter,

Things aren't as we expected, are they? When you were surrounded by the comforts of the womb, you never anticipated gas pains, medical tests, or sun in your eyes. Nor did I anticipate a baby who didn't go by the "books," a baby who was put together a little differently than others.

There is no diagnosis, nor predictions regarding your future. So innocent you are. You don't care that you can't lift your head or make eye contact with people. You're happy just the way you are.

That's good enough for now. And "now" is all that really concerns me at this point. I live one day at a time—enjoying you and loving you.

Kathryn, you're good for me.

CHAPTER FIFTEEN

THE AMAZING JOURNEYS OF THREE OTHER PARENTS

One of my hopes in writing this book is that you won't feel quite so alone in your parenting journey. Oh, how I would have benefited from the Internet when Kathryn was a baby! In the early days especially, I longed to connect with other parents who had children with intellectual and developmental differences. Over the years I've discovered that no matter how diverse we are, what we all seem to have in common is a fierce love for and commitment to our children. When I think of committed parents, I think of the parents you are about to meet: Dawn, Vanessa, and John, along with his wife Carol. I have the greatest respect for these parents, and I hope their stories touch you as much as they touched me.

DAWN

The year was 1997 and my mother, who was accompanying me as she often did back then to various appointments, was sitting with me in the DEC (Developmental Evaluation Center) on what seemed to be an otherwise random day. My son Cody was approaching his third birthday and we (his dad, my mom, and I) had been taking him to this center several times per week since he was approximately 15 months old. We were under the guidance of Cody's pediatrician, Dr. Sarah Hudson, and his neurodevelopmental specialist, Dr. Thomas Montgomery (not quite the same thing as neurologist; Dr. Montgomery would affectionately tell us he needed one more class to have become a neurologist and he didn't get that class!).

Dr. Hudson had been Cody's doctor since I gave birth to him. She was the first doctor to see him in routine rounds at the hospital. Over the last three years, she had become increasingly concerned about how he was developing, as he was missing his milestones. She referred us to Dr. Montgomery, a colleague whom she felt could give us additional help and resources in determining what was causing Cody to be what they referred to as "developmentally delayed." For the first 12 months of his life, we waited to see Cody's skills emerge. There was no other obvious cause for concern. My pregnancy and delivery were completely normal, with no complications. Cody had no physical condition or clear abnormalities that pointed to him being anything but a healthy little boy. With that said, he was not making his milestones on time, often being very behind in achieving them (i.e., holding his head on his own, getting into a sit position by himself, walking, and talking), or not achieving them at all. So we waited during that first year.

By the second year, Dr. Hudson said we needed to be more active in investigating this matter to try and ascertain the cause of his delays. Hence, we were referred to Dr. Montgomery. We also started going to the DEC during this same time. At DEC, Cody received physical therapy, occupational therapy, and speech therapy to help improve his "global" delays. We saw a small bit of progress with Cody in these areas, but nothing that really stood out as a breakthrough. The therapists were all very professional, caring, and quite affectionate toward him. They definitely engaged with Cody as much as he would allow them to.

But, back to the random day and the appointment with my mother. On this day, I believe we were seeing the psychiatrist. I am honestly not sure of his title. All I remember of the day was sitting in his office and my very wise, intuitive mother asking this gentleman, "When should we expect Cody to catch up with his peers?" He calmly and assuredly answered, "He will not catch up with his peers."

Wait, he won't catch up, as in never? I thought. No one had said that in over the last almost three years. This revelation hit me like a ton of bricks. Was I supposed to know this from the doctors and specialists who advised us that our son was "developmentally delayed"?

After a good cry, I thought about what this meant for Cody. Up until that point, part of me actually believed I could "pencil in" a date that Cody would start to walk, talk, interact more, play imitation games such as peek-a-boo— to do all the things the baby book was saying he should be doing, or should have done some time ago.

This was obviously not the start of my journey with Cody. However, it was the first day I started to realize in a more profound and direct way that his journey was not going to be what I had planned or envisioned. For any parent this awareness is heavy. And it was certainly heavy for me. All we wanted as Cody's parents was for our boy to be loved and accepted. Although we would love and accept him, if he were truly different, would he ever be loved and accepted by others? What would his life be like in five years, 10 years, 20 years from now?

And now for the glimmer of hope: During the same time the doctor told us that Cody was too far behind and by all indications would not catch up with his peers, I picked up a magazine that lay on a table in the DEC's waiting room. The receptionist said I could take the magazine home if I wanted. "Okay," I thought. Little did I realize it had a poem on the back that has stuck with me to this day—one that greatly encouraged me. Had the receptionist known this when she told me I could take the copy home with me?

The poem was titled "Random Reflections on a Vest" and was written by Tim Weiss. It was on the back cover of the magazine. I no longer have the magazine, but I did manage to hang on to the back cover. Here is the poem in its entirety:

Random Reflections on a Vest
by Tim Weiss

A coat without arms is a vest.
Not a broken coat with a disability.
It is just different.

It may have trouble alone in some environments,
like the snow,
But do better than a coat in other situations or
environments.
You can't cure a vest; it isn't sick or broken.
It is different.
Minor alterations can be made—but only if appropriate.
If you have the skill, or can find someone
with sufficient skills, it may function better.
But it is still a vest.
You do not regret that it is a vest because it is not a coat.
You accept it.
You wear it.
You take care of it so it will last a long, long time.

What healing these words brought to me! I still cannot read it without choking up a little. It is simple, but it covers all the ground. Cody is not broken; he is a unique person formed in the image of God. He will need help, so I must look for those with sufficient skills to help him. Mostly, I must accept Cody. I must let him be Cody. I must let him live the life that he desires to live, help him to do so, and be his biggest champion and supporter along the way.

Cody is now 29 years old, so a lot of time has passed since that day at the DEC office. Cody has never received an actual diagnosis. On paper, he tests in the range of severe IDD. What this means is we know what range he tests in, but we have no idea why that is so. What made Cody be the person he is? What made him be—in comparison to the rest of the population—in the "less than one-tenth of one percent"? I always wondered why they couldn't have just said he was in the less than one percent of the population. It is hard to fully understand what less than one-tenth of one percent means ...

In search of answers, Cody has undergone all genetic testing available. All results have come back negative. While he was growing and developing, his pediatrician would say to me many times, "Dawn, he is his own syndrome."

Cody is classified as nonverbal. He does not speak, at least not in terms of traditional language/verbal communication. However, he can say a very limited number of words. He can say, recognizably, approximately 20 words. He predominately uses about five or six words on a daily basis. I sometimes forget he can say more words, but then he will randomly say a word I haven't heard in a while. I am pleasantly surprised when this happens, and tell him what a great job he is doing. He says "o hat" each day. "O hat" is pertaining to any round object he sees—and also it could refer to an actual hat. He says "orange" for his favorite Sunkist drink. He says "go up" to share with me his love for all things that have a motion of going up or are upward in structure (e.g., garage doors, elevators, and bridges). He says "pipe" every day and is intrigued by plumbing material.

His favorite thing on earth to do is to ride in the car. He particularly likes going over bridges (as mentioned) and he also likes going through the car wash. He likes going to his doctor's appointments. He is fascinated with medical equipment and particularly likes patient beds, as he enjoys watching them go up and down.

Two-thirds of each month, Cody is at home with my husband and me. My husband, Cody's stepfather, loves Cody as his own. I know it must not have been easy for my husband to take on this responsibility, but he has. He does not complain and he is not bitter about it. He assists on every level and truly is a helpmate to me for Cody. They share a special bond and I am grateful for the both of us that my husband is a part of this journey.

During his time at home, Cody enjoys watching YouTube videos of things he likes (such as, but not limited to, cars going over bridges, cars going through car washes, garage doors, garage door installations, senior citizen line dancing groups, *The Price Is Right,* and live performances—he has been really hooked on Michael McDonald and Neil Diamond lately, but he enjoys almost all musical artists). He listens to the radio and plays with vinyl records (he doesn't listen to the vinyl records, but instead enjoys holding them and placing them in their jacket). He also likes plumbing catalog books, Toy Story books, and the chunky wooden puzzles.

The remaining part of the month, Cody stays at a respite house about an hour and a half away. He visits an adult day center during his respite stay. He enjoys being with his friends, and we get good reports of him being happy during his stays. His respite stays give both my husband and me respite time, while also giving Cody the ability to experience things other than being at home.

Cody's father is no longer here on earth with him. Cody had his father in his life for almost 25 years; his dad passed away suddenly a few weeks' shy of Cody's twenty-fifth birthday. Cody's father loved him with his whole heart and was a wonderful father to him. Cody loved to go for rides with his daddy. I can't help but think Cody remembers that. Since Cody does not understand death, my husband and I have never told him that his father passed way. I think Cody sees it as being physically away from one another, without having to feel any sting of grief associated with losing someone he loves dearly. Coming to the realization that Cody will not have to experience grief is not something I wanted to learn. Despite this being the case, I am extremely thankful for the fact he does not have to experience that type of pain.

Cody has come a long way since his developmental childhood years and teenage years. That time frame—from approximately 10 years old through late teens into early adulthood—was the most challenging time period for my family. Cody would have behavioral outbursts that could be physical. They did not happen every day, but could occur several times a week. t could be very intense at times when the outbursts were really bad. The worst time for us was the teenage years. During this time, Cody continued to love to ride. However, we were unable to transition him back into the house after riding. Car rides could easily take up to eight hours at a time, and even after that long period of riding we still struggled to get him back into our home. Safety was a huge concern. With the help of a neurologist, we were able to medicate Cody during car rides and successfully get him back into our home. His dad and I together carried him into the house while he was in a deep sleep. I purchased a loveseat that opened into a bed to make it easier for us. He had gained weight during that season, I am assuming from many of the medicines he was taking, and so carrying him into the house and placing him on that pop-out bed was truly an act of love. This was a time of our life when we coped the very best we could. This season did pass, thankfully, and Cody's behavior and ability to transition is greatly improved. He still needs medical intervention to help him, but we have been able to lower the dosage and even discontinue some of the medicines previously used.

The advice I would give to a young parent of a child with special needs is to have a clear understanding of what the term "developmentally delayed" means, especially if they are hearing this a lot through the formative years. I perceived the term "delayed" as something temporary and not necessarily permanent. Without having an actual diagnosis, I thought Cody would still be able to catch up with his peers. I did not fully understand the term. I do not blame anyone for this; it is just something I now (having hindsight) may have pursued differently. Perhaps I should have asked more questions about that term, or asked different questions. When a doctor uses the term, they may not realize how the parent is receiving it. A parent is innately going to have hope. For me, I attached a strong sense of hope to the term and, at least in my mind, perceived it to automatically mean temporary when in fact it was not.

I would encourage a parent with a special needs child to always advocate for their child. No one will know or understand their child's needs the way they know and understand their child's needs. I have no specific advice as it relates to advocacy because every situation is unique. I would also tell you that it is okay to grieve not having a typical journey. Your feelings of loss as it relates to this are real and valid. It hurts to know your child is going to have a different path than others. There is nothing shameful in recognizing that hurt and giving oneself grace as it relates to this. I would also point out that people are going to say things to you out of a lack of knowledge on their part and as it relates to their own child's condition. When this occurs, give the other person grace. I feel convinced that, except on the very rare occasion when someone is truly just a jerk, people do mean well. If you can use the encounter as a teachable moment, do so. With that said, don't always feel like you have to learn from every encounter—you will get exhausted if so. Lastly and above all else, I would tell you to accept your child for the beautiful soul that they are because their souls are light and their hearts possess an innocence that is so very rare. We are the lucky ones to ever encounter such beauty.

VANESSA

"Mrs. McNear, there is something wrong with your baby's brain and I need to do an amniocentesis immediately." Those words forever changed our lives. Prior to that day, we were living in bliss about being pregnant again. Maddox would be joining his three siblings, all a good amount older than he, and we couldn't be happier. But on the day of my Level 2 ultrasound, because of my age (I was 36), they wanted a better look. I will never forget how cold the doctor was. She didn't say anything while doing the ultrasound. Normally you get the standard, "There's your baby's heart, fingers, toes," etc. But not a word was uttered until she said she needed to do an amniocentesis. After performing the amniocentesis, a genetic counselor came in and said to me, "This is not the baby you want." She said that I should consider an abortion immediately. I asked what they had found on the ultrasound, and she said my baby had severe hydrocephalus. I asked her what that meant, and she told me it meant his head was filled with fluid and most of the time, babies with hydrocephalus do not survive birth.

I was then told they would call me with the results from the amniocentesis the next day and I could decide from there. I asked her how she could possibly know what kind of baby I wanted, and I left the room. My mother-in-law was with me, and the two of us just looked at each other in shock—shock at how unprofessional the doctor was, shock at how heartless the genetic counselor was, and shock at all that had just taken place.

Before this appointment, Maddox was the easiest pregnancy. There had been no morning sickness, no sitting on a nerve. It was just easy—easy until that day. Then it was replaced with so much anxiety, fear, and uncertainty. For the next 19 weeks and a few days, all I did was worry and try to fix it. I even sent an email to a doctor that had conducted research using large amounts of folic acid on mice with hydrocephalus. I asked him how much he gave the mice so I could try and treat myself to fix Maddox. Now looking back, I wish I had just enjoyed being pregnant. It was my last pregnancy, and the joy was taken away from me. The doctor who told me, "This is not the baby you want," was not the person I wanted to deal with. One of my best friends works in the medical field and called a high-risk OB she knew to see if he would see me. It was almost like God laid everything out. That doctor had just started to accept my insurance the day before, and they had an appointment the next day in the morning and could see me. This doctor was the complete opposite of the first one. He took about two hours doing an ultrasound and looked at every inch of Maddox. He told my husband and me that everything looked good minus the hydrocephalus. He then made appointments for me to get an MRI, genetic testing, and blood work. The MRI showed there were no obstructions or tumors. Genetic testing came back with no abnormalities. Blood work always came back good. All he could tell us was that we wouldn't know how bad it was until the baby was born and shunted because everyone is different and their bodies respond differently.

We arrived at the hospital for my C-section due to Maddox's head measuring 42 cm. I was really nervous and my doctor warned me that I needed to calm down or they wouldn't be able to do the surgery because my blood pressure was so high. Maddox was born on July 14, 2009, shortly after 8:00 a.m. I remember wanting to hear him cry because that would be a sign he was a fighter. And there it was, the most amazing, beautiful cry ever. My husband was able to hold Maddox while they put me back together and he brought him to me to see. He was the most perfect-looking baby. I started to think the doctors had been wrong and all our prayers had been answered. Maddox had a ventriculoperitoneal (VP) shunt (a cerebral shunt) placed three days after birth. It was hard to see him in pain from the surgery, but we knew he needed it to get the pressure relieved from pushing his brain up against his skull. Maddox did really well with the surgery, and on the tenth day after he was born, he was moved down to the Level 3 NICU. He had his first seizure that day and was quickly put back in the Level 4 NICU. They had him hooked up to the EEG equipment to monitor his seizures and began to treat him with phenobarbital. He kept having seizures and that was when the doctors wanted to have a meeting with us. I will never forget sitting in the conference room with around 12 other people, all with their different opinions of what was wrong with Maddox. This is when we knew it was more than hydrocephalus. We were given a whole list of different diagnoses: blind, epileptic, cerebral palsy, encephalitis, and most likely a genetic condition called Walker-Warburg. We were told that even though the shunt had drained fluid, his brain had not "bounced back" like they had hoped it would, so he had a very small outer rim of brain and brain stem. They really pushed the Walker-Warburg diagnosis even though we had done the genetic testing, and they told us not to expect him to live past age three. The best thing we could do was to take him home and love him until his time came. We were both crushed about our sweet, strong little boy. Why?!?!?

We decided that day that we would take him home and love him and do absolutely everything to make him the best Maddox he could be. After spending about three and a half more weeks in the hospital and beginning another medicine for seizure control, Maddox got to come home. We were so scared. Our other children just did what kids do and played with him. My daughter loved to play with him when he was little. She would sometimes put make up on him and bows in his hair, and he loved it, because his sissy was paying attention to him. My oldest son was a little taken back by the situation. He was almost old enough to have kids of his own and I think the fear of everything scared him. My other son was super protective of him. If anyone said anything negative about him, he immediately put them in their place. And that was just the beginning.

We began the journey of many doctors, specialists, therapies, and medical equipment. And we were terribly overwhelmed. We felt all alone. It put a strain on our marriage. The constant appointments and more diagnoses and more medicine. But Maddox was doing great. He seemed like a normal baby—eating, pooping, sleeping, laughing, playing, growing. We took him to Duke University Medical Center for a stem cell infusion after researching how amazing stem cells were. Of course like everything else, different people experienced different responses. It did help with his seizures, and I will always be thankful and grateful for that.

Maddox started school and loved every minute of it. But that is also when he started to get sick, a lot—everything from colds, to stomach bugs and then hand, foot, and mouth disease. That was a very scary week in the hospital with many doctors not knowing what to do while also trying to do some really risky stuff with him. That was also the beginning of me not backing down with the doctors and insisting they listen to me and his regular doctors that know him. He finished his first year of school, and the summer came and went and he started his next year.

After fewer than two weeks he got sick again. He had an upper respiratory infection that turned into pneumonia. After two to three months of getting a little better, then getting sick again, changing medicine, and even a short three-day hospital admission only to get sick again, we went to the doctor to have a check-up to make sure he was getting better. The nurse came in to get his vitals and then disappeared, saying she would be back in a minute. The next thing I knew, I was being ushered out of the room and the person next to me was asking me how to reach my husband. All the doctors in the office were running into Maddox's room and I heard, "Crash cart, epinephrine." It was surreal and unbelievable. We were rushed to the hospital, and I was told Life Flight was enroute to pick Maddox up. While all the doctors in the ER were working on him, he coded in front of me. Again, surreal. I remember seeing the nurse climb on top of him, giving my little baby chest compressions. I said, "You're hurting him!" and she said, "No, I am saving his life."

He came back and then coded again. They were able to get him back and then Life Flight showed up and took over. He was transported via helicopter to Texas Children's Hospital. When we arrived, we waited for five-plus hours before we could see him. We were told he had coded multiple times on the helicopter as well as when he arrived, but they didn't give up. He had pneumonia and a urinary tract infection. He was intubated and had a chest tube coming out of his side. He looked horrible. He had so many wires and tubes and machines. But he was alive and still fighting. We were able to come home on New Year's Eve. It was awesome, but this was just the start of many, many hospital visits over the years. He is now G-tube fed due to aspiration risks. He literally can aspirate on his own spit and then get pneumonia.

When all the hospital admissions began, I started to feel like I couldn't handle keeping him healthy and alive on my own. We have been very fortunate to have the same nurse from the beginning, and she is literally his lifesaver. She knows every little bit of him and I always joke that even when Maddox farts wrong she is on top of it and either aggressively doing extra treatments, giving extra medicines, etc., or calling the doctor ahead of time to tell them we are on our way to the ER.

A few weeks after Maddox turned nine years old, he got sick again and it was even worse than the last time. He was admitted with RSV, was intubated, and was able to pull through. But then his PICC line became infected and that was when things got really scary. He became septic and had meningitis along with some sort of horrible bacteria called Serratia marcescens. It ended up infecting his shunt which caused a brain infection. His first brain surgery was to remove his shunt due to the raging infection in his brain. I still remember seeing the physician's assistant from neurosurgery tapping his shunt and seeing what they took out. Spinal fluid should only be clear. His looked yellow and had puss and blood floating around in it. I knew right away this was not good. The second surgery they performed was to remove a cyst filled with puss that was pushing up against his brain stem. The third brain surgery was to take the cyst out again (it kept filling up with puss) and clean up all the infection. I truly thought we would lose him. I had to get a team of doctors to back me up because one of the doctors tending to him wanted to send him home on hospice.

All his doctors came and backed me up. And after four surgeries and 114 days in the PICU, we came home. This stay wasn't only hard on Maddox, but on my other kids. They were older by then and understood more, but they still needed Mom to be home and I couldn't be. But like I told them, I would do the same for them if they were sick. I remember being there in the PICU just longing to be home doing mundane things like cleaning, cooking, listening to my other children argue, and doing laundry (who misses laundry?!). But after watching Maddox fight and having to fight for him, normalcy is what we wanted.

Since this time, Maddox has had two more surgeries—one to replace his GI tube and then another brain surgery when the cyst came back. Today I can honestly say he has never been better. He has stayed healthy and happy. What more can I ask for? He has been a fighter from the start and he continues to be. He is and always will be the strongest person I know and continues to defy the odds that were put against him over 14 years ago. He will be 15 this July and will be starting the 10th grade. I wish all those doctors in that conference room could see him now. What we strive for now is not to have an extraordinary life, but to have an extra ordinary one filled with sitting on the couch and having snuggly time and laughing at silly sounds.

Never let doctors put limits on your child, and always be your child's voice. They have so much to say if you just listen.

JOHN

John and his wife, Carol, live with their 40-year-old son Jarred in California. They are his court-appointed conservators, as I was with Kathryn. They are also his primary caretakers. Their two younger children are now adults and no longer live at home. The services at Jarred's day program were terminated in June 2018 because they were no longer able to provide adequate support for Jarred's health and safety as well as the health and safety of the staff and other clients. Since John and Carol haven't been able to locate a new local day program that can meet Jarred's needs, he has been at home full time for over five years now.

Jarred has no verbal communication, safety awareness, or self-care skills so he requires 24-hour protective supervision and assistance. He is able to communicate through picture identification, leading by hand, body gestures, and other sound effects.

Jarred's disability was not immediately known when he was born. It was not until he was about three to four months old that Carol called the doctor's attention to Jarred's "delayed head control." Their primary care physician did not seem to have any urgent concern, but Carol's growing sense of unease led to the beginning of a battery of tests and consultations over the next several years. During this time, Jarred was "diagnosed" by various doctors with gross motor delay (1983), global developmental delay (1984), pervasive developmental disorder (1989), and severe mental retardation (1991).

In the first eight years, Jarred received several medical workups to gain a better understanding of his disabilities. Magnetic Resonance Imaging scans and Computerized Tomography scans were within normal limits. Genetic testing did not reveal any abnormalities with his chromosomes either. Regardless of the terms given by the medical community, it felt like an "un-diagnosis" to John and Carol because the medical team gave no answers, no solutions, nor future prognosis. They felt trapped in an indeterminate state.

Although Jarred has never officially been diagnosed with autism, he exhibits several tendencies indicative of autistic behavior, so when they are in social settings with people unfamiliar to them, they often refer to Jarred's diagnosis as autism. Because autism is readily understood and recognized by the public, it's easier to refer to it than to go into a long-winded explanation about why he might be having a behavior issue. Sometimes Jarred has explosive outbursts in public, so they have found that using the word autism helps in these situations.

With friends, family, and within the disability culture, they use "intellectual disability for unknown reasons," unknown being the operative word as his disability is unexplained neurologically or genetically.

Regarding the early days, John says, "In many ways, Jarred seemed like a healthy baby boy. Carol returned to work about three months after Jarred was born so we split parenting duties while the other one worked, avoiding day care.

"I know there was a significant amount of anxiety for my wife. This might be an overstatement, but she was almost consumed with worry and thoughts of blame, as in 'What did I do wrong?' and 'What could I have done differently?' My personality tends to react to challenges or crises with a very analytical response. I am sure I had my angry moments, but I accepted the severity of the situation, provided the necessary emotional support, and remained positive while looking for the next logical step. It may sound very detached, but it has been a useful survival method.

"I recall both of us wanting to find an answer, a reason, a definitive diagnosis. The term 'unknown reason' seemed inadequate with too wide a range of possibilities, leaving us open to doubting ourselves and wondering whether we had done something wrong to cause Jarred's condition. There seemed to be a point in time where we were fixated on finding a reason. We spent many days in meetings and at medical appointments looking for answers. In part, we wanted answers regarding an identifiable cause which could have an impact on our plans to have additional children. Even with no known genetic cause attached to Jarred's disability, subsequent pregnancies were at best anxious moments.

"Handling Jarred when he was younger required constant effort, but because of his size and age, it was easier than it is today. Many of his early behaviors remain but have become larger in scale, more destructive, and harder to control, primarily because of his increase in size and strength. As a child, simply holding him in our arms until the behavior passed had a more nurturing, protective parenting feeling.

"Jarred's baseline behavior has always contained some form of underlying agitation, typically vocalization or chewing on his clothing. Additionally, he is extremely sensitive to any change in his routine or with the people he interacts with. Consequently, the activities you would typically associate with raising a child are different. Jarred didn't do team sports, he didn't have school friends coming over to the house to play or sleep over. His communication deficit was a barrier to developing friendships outside of his immediate family because it was difficult for others (in particular, his peers) to understand him.

"Instead, we found other local activities that entertained him. His grandma made it her mission to ensure Jarred regularly attended live performances at the local community theater where he made friends with the cast members. We all did things that provided him with the greatest enjoyment on his terms—always on his terms."

When I asked John what helped him and his wife to get through the early days, he said, "I remember when Jarred was about eight or nine years old, we made a conscious decision to stop all the testing and searching for answers. Jarred was intellectually disabled for unknown reasons and that was that. Continued testing was as frustrating for Jarred as it was for us. While there are several reasons for wanting to understand the cause and have an identifiable diagnosis, it just was not going to happen for Jarred. Making the decision to refocus our energies to moving forward with what we did know provided a greater sense of control and responsibility for Jarred's future.

"At about this same time, I was fortunate to have been provided a volunteer opportunity with a large international nonprofit organization that merged Jarred's intellectual disability with my law enforcement career. [Editor's note: John is now retired from a 30-year law enforcement career.] Local events were family inclusive and provided Jarred opportunities to be successful at his level in an environment where he was socially accepted. This opportunity developed a foundational coping mechanism for me because this was now the community in which we didn't need to explain anything. I identified and found acceptance for Jarred's disability."

What helps John and Carol now is knowing that Jarred is in a safe environment and loved in their home. They know that they have done everything they can to ensure his well-being. They do a lot of preplanning and use environmental control to give Jarred his greatest chance at success.

They've found that they really need to be in tune with what Jarred is doing and to the subtle cues that need to be identified and acted upon quickly.

John says, "The greatest help I get is from Carol. This is true for both of us. We give each other personal time to reenergize when needed, and we use respite care in order to get out and spend time together at least once a month. Maintaining some sense of normalcy in our relation has been important. We also recognize those things we cannot change and find ways to incorporate our situation into the mainstream to maintain our emotional health."

When asked about what advice he wishes someone had given him when their child was born, John says, "Don't wait. Educate yourself now about all aspects of raising and living with a special needs child. While you may understandably be focused on immediate needs, look ahead to adulthood.

"Be persistent; your child's best advocate is you. Look into Early Intervention Services, health care, Social Security, Regional Center Services, conservatorship, Medi-Cal (if you reside in California), Medicaid, parent support groups, Lanterman Developmental Disabilities Services Act (California), Individuals with Disabilities Education Act (Federal), financial planning (and these are just a few of many).

"No one ever knocked on our door and said, 'Here is everything you need to know, and we would like to offer you all these services.' We discovered a lot of this along the way and sometimes I had to ramp up my knowledge quickly to ensure services were provided.

"Researching, locating, and accessing effective resources is a continuous, time-consuming process. It has been my experience that many of the municipal, county, state, and federal agencies mandated to support persons with disabilities are overwhelmed, underfunded, or unprepared. Again, I go back to: be persistent; your child's best advocate is you.

"An example that reoccurs quite often is that Jarred's behavior creates unique challenges when attempting to obtain medical care within a system that is unprepared to receive patients who do not fit the typical procedures for patient care. This often results in numerous lengthy phone calls or office visits to preplan a medical appointment and just get in the door. We have made it abundantly clear to everyone in the medical system that Jarred is intellectually disabled with autistic-like characteristics and requires special consideration to avoid these agitated states when seeking medical services. It hasn't sunk in yet.

As Carol and I get older, coping with the emotional and physical demands of caring for Jarred weighs on us. As I mentioned, his size and strength have increased and it has becoming increasingly hard to control the behaviors. Additional in-home care assistant options are limited because of his behavior, as the resource pool at this level is almost nonexistent. This would be true of a group care facility also. We are frequently reminded that there will come a time when Jarred will have to transition to a different living arrangement.

"Speak up, ask questions, don't be intimidated or embarrassed. Applaud the smallest accomplishments and believe in yourself."

Lastly, I asked John what some of the rewards have been from this unplanned journey of theirs, and this was his response:

"I think there is a tendency to get caught up in all the daily challenges of caring for Jarred. No doubt it is all-consuming, but it's hard to imagine it any other way. There are many rewarding personal moments—the cheer that goes up when he completes a puzzle, his version of singing along to a music video, a giggle while turning the pages of a book, his hugs, and his absolute delight while visiting Disneyland or when Santa visits our house.

"Jarred's disability has provided my family and me with a greater understanding, compassion, patience, and respect for all people with disabilities. I have been provided with many unique experiences, and many special people have been brought into our lives because I had a child with a disability."

CHAPTER SIXTEEN

PARTING GIFTS: SAYING GOODBYE TO MY GIRL

Those we love and lose are always connected
by heartstrings into infinity.
— Terri Guillemets

In March 2023, Kathryn was given a new diagnosis: Stage 4 inflammatory carcinoma and Stage 4 Triple Negative breast cancer, i.e., terminal breast cancer. I felt as though a Mack truck was barreling down the road my daughter was on, and I was helpless to get her out of the way. Once again, fear, sadness, and confusion flooded my heart and mind. I found myself on a new journey, and I didn't like where this one was headed. Suddenly I found myself back in those stages of grief I talked about in Chapter Four.

Kathryn's favorite thing in life besides gummy bears and her beloved Mozart Magic Cube was going for car rides.

Needless to say, her sister Ann and I were there to give her as many rides as possible. Those memories are sacred to me now. And then the succession of dreaded "lasts" began: the last time she was able to walk to the car, her last car ride, the last time she ate solids, and her last breath.

The hospice organization we chose couldn't have been more amazing. From the director to the chaplain, each person was like a superhero. I'll forever be grateful for their expertise, guidance, and support.

Being Kathryn's mother taught me how to hold both joy and sorrow at the same time. In that sense, that was her parting gift to me. Being her mother gave me the strength to bear losing her. And despite the excruciating sadness of her passing, her sister and I also experienced immense joy in knowing that our girl was set free from the brain and body that limited her so for 31 years.

While Kathryn was labeled as "profoundly disabled," in a sense she lived life profoundly on her own terms. And that is how she passed—peacefully, by herself, on her beloved bed in her beloved room. We know that is how she would have wanted it.

Kathryn's "perfectly imperfect" theme made one more appearance at her Celebration of Life service. Leading up to the big event, I hounded Ann to make sure that all the technological details for the service were in order. I had assembled carefully curated songs to be played as people arrived and other meaningful songs to be played after the service. The shining star of the service was to be a chronological video of Kathryn's life that was also set to music. To say that I was stressed about all of this being perfectly orchestrated was an understatement. Once again, it was a matter of "By golly, I couldn't control my daughter's cancer, but you better believe I'm controlling every element of her Celebration of Life service!" I brought everything on a thumb drive to the funeral home several days ahead of time to make sure that all was in working order. They assured me that everything worked perfectly.

Fast forward to the service. Not only were the songs all jumbled up, but they played over the soundtrack of the video as well—the video that got stuck before Kathryn was even eight years old. My greatest fear became a reality, and what was my response? I just looked at Ann and smiled, and then laughed. We all laughed. So palpable was the love in that room that none of these technical details mattered. It was a perfect moment.

Love ruled, and everything else took a back seat. Many people said it was the most beautiful memorial service they had ever attended. That was when I felt Kathryn's greatest gift of all to me: that deep sense of knowing that love trumps all. We can try our hardest to do everything just so, but in the end, it's the love and caring that makes the difference in our lives.

Thirty-one years ago when I gave birth to Kathryn, I couldn't possibly understand that she would end up being the greatest blessing of my life, but she was. Despite missing her like crazy, I now revel in knowing that she has crossed the finish line of the "Life on Earth Marathon." Her work here was done, and I know we will one day be reunited, and what a reunion that will be!

If you should lose your beloved child, I cannot stress enough the importance of being gentle with yourself during all the ups and downs you will be going through. Remember that everyone reacts to loss in his or her own personal way.

A dear friend shared with me that in the beginning, you go through a time where you can hardly believe your loved one is gone. It's like getting a cut on your hand where you see the blood flowing, but the extent of the pain hasn't registered yet.

When a loved one passes, there may be a brief time before the full impact of the pain hits you. Sometimes it isn't until after the funeral or memorial service that the impact of your loss is felt. It is important to know that the grief will ease in time. It's as if the wound begins to heal, and you are able to live and laugh once again. But even when the wound is healed, a scar remains, and pain can pop up at the most unexpected times. You may see a child who reminds you of yours, or a song you listened to together comes on the radio, or a memory pops up on Facebook. You'll find that along with the pain is joy as well though—the joy of having loved so fully and so unconditionally. As I mentioned earlier, it is possible to hold both sadness and joy at the same time, and with time, joy and gratitude will reign.

CONCLUSION

If there's one tool you take from this book more than any other, let it be this: the benefit of making modifications. Let me explain by sharing an analogy.

Years ago I was convinced that Pilates wasn't for me. As much as I admired the insanely fit bodies of the Pilates enthusiasts I knew, when they talked about how good Pilates was for their core strength and their abs, it sounded more painful than promising. My philosophy was more along the lines of "Life's short; why torture yourself?" Then I tried a class, and I became hooked. How did *that* happen, you might ask?

The reason can be summed up in one word: modifications. The instructor told us that whether you were a quadriplegic or just miserably out of shape, in Pilates there are modifications to make each exercise doable for you. It turned out, the instructor was right. She made all the exercises doable for me, and in doing so, I eventually achieved a level of strength and flexibility I didn't even know was possible for me.

This principle of "modifications" was key as Kathryn's mother. In the beginning I thought there was no way I could survive changing my daughter's diapers for the rest of her life or quitting work indefinitely in order to care for her. However, because of resources and options and making modifications that made sense to me, I was able to be the very best mother I could be for my beloved daughter. Modifications made it possible for me to live true to myself while watching Kathryn live her best life as well.

As I began to recognize my triggers in those early days of parenting, I began to modify like crazy! For example, the first couple of Thanksgivings were tough because my water broke with Kathryn after Thanksgiving dinner. This brought up very difficult memories in the early years after Kathryn's birth. That was when our Thanksgiving at Disneyland tradition began!

I encourage you to keep this in mind as you start out on this new journey. The next time you decide something is too daunting, too painful, too expensive, or just too anything, consider modifying whatever it is to make it doable for you.

There is a way to navigate this journey that will be right for you. You may wish to care for your child at home for as long as you live or you may choose to place him or her in a group home setting at a point in time that feels right to you. Only you will know the best solution for your child and family, and you shouldn't allow anyone else to tell you otherwise. There is no right or wrong solution; it is whatever makes the most sense at any given time. Allow yourself to grow in wisdom along this journey, accept your limitations, and seek to always act from a place of love and compassion.

The term "special needs" is no longer a tragic designation to me. It's something that brings all of us parents together—that desire to identify the unique needs of our child, whether his I.Q. is 50 or 150. It's about parenting in such a way that whatever your child's abilities, he will use them to make a contribution on this earth. While I never experienced Kathryn auditioning for her school play or heading off for college, I also never had to worry about her coming in late from a date or anguish over her not making the cheerleading squad. At the end of her life, I ended up celebrating all that made her my one-of-a-kind daughter, and I couldn't have been prouder had she been the first female President of the United States.

Lastly, on one of our Thanksgiving-at-Disneyland trips, the worker in their special needs nursery gave me a piece written by Erma Bombeck. I hope it touches you as much as it touched me. Although Ms. Bombeck wrote this for mothers, it applies to fathers as well.

The Special Mother
by Erma Bombeck

Did you ever wonder how mothers of disabled children were chosen? Somehow I visualize God hovering over the earth selecting his instruments of propagation with great care and deliberation.

As He observes, He instructs His angels to make notes in a giant ledger.

"This one gets a daughter. The Patron saint will be Cecelia."

"This one gets twins. The Patron saint will be Matthew."

"This one gets a son. The Patron saint . . . give her Gerard. He's used to profanity."

Finally He passes a name to an angel and smiles. "Give her a disabled child."

The angel is curious. "Why this one, God? She's so happy"

"Exactly," smiles God. "Could I give a disabled child to a mother who does not know laughter? That would be cruel!"

"But has she patience?" asks the angel.

"I don't want her to have too much patience or she will drown in a sea of sorrow and despair. Once the shock and resentment wear off, she'll handle it.

"I watched her today. She has that feeling of self and independence that is so necessary in a mother. You see, the child I'm going to give her has his own world. She has to make him live in her world and that's not going to be easy."

"But Lord, I don't think she even believes in you."

God smiles. "No matter, I can fix that. This one is perfect—she has just enough selfishness."

The angel gasps. "Selfishness? Is that a virtue?"

God nods. "If she can't separate herself from the child occasionally, she won't survive. Yes, here is a woman whom I will bless with a child less than perfect.

"She doesn't realize it yet, but she is to be envied. She will never take for granted a 'spoken word.' She will never consider any 'step' ordinary. When her child says 'Momma' for the first time she will be present at a miracle and will know it. I will permit her to see clearly the things I see ... ignorance, cruelty and prejudice . . . and allow her to rise above them.

"She will never be alone. I will be at her side every minute of every day of her life because she is doing my work as surely as if she is here by my side."

"And what about her Patron saint?" asks the angel, his pen poised in midair. God smiles. "A mirror will suffice."[23]

HELPFUL WEBSITES
(IN ALPHABETICAL ORDER)

- American Academy of Pediatrics provides an online service for parents to find appropriate doctors and dentists in their geographical locations: www.aap.org.

- The American College of Emergency Physicians and the American Academy of Pediatrics have created an Emergency Information Form for Children with Special Health Care Needs that you can download from their website: www.acep.org. Having this document with you will assure that your child will receive the most prompt and appropriate medical care possible.

- The Arc – A disability rights organization that works with and for people with IDD, their families, and their communities: www.thearc.org.

- For information on respite care in your state, visit the ARCH (National Respite Network). Their website is https://archrespite.org/. http://chtop.org/ARCH.html.

- www.Befreeco.com is a line of adaptive clothing founded by moms.

- Centers for Disease Control and Prevention provides information on developmental milestones, and their website is CDC.gov.

- Center for Parent Information and Resources (CPIR) is a good source for learning about specific disabilities. Their website is ParentCenterHub.org. They offer information on the full spectrum of disabilities in children, including developmental delays and rare disorders. On their site, you can find links to learn about typical developmental milestones in childhood as well as information on identifying and treating specific disabilities and disorders.

- At Childcare.gov, you can explore your state's resources that are available to you such as childcare, health and social services, financial assistance, and more.

- Children's Hospitals. Most large metropolitan areas have a children's hospital, and you can do an online search for one near you at www.childrenshospitals.org.

- Disabled World provides information on famous people and celebrities with disabilities. www.disabled-world.com

- The Individuals with Disabilities Education Act (IDEA) governs how states and public agencies provide early intervention, special education, and related services to more than 7.5 million eligible infants, toddlers, children, and youth with disabilities. Their website provides information for each state: https://sites.ed.gov/idea/.

- The National Center for Complementary and Integrative Health website, https://www.nccih.nih.gov/, is a very credible source when you are researching alternative medicine.

- Shriners Children's Hospitals may be found at www.shrinerschildrens.org/en. They provide nonprofit medical facilities across North American for children with orthopedic conditions, burns, spinal cord injuries, and cleft lip and palates, regardless of the patients' ability to pay.

- The Social Security Administration provides information on SSI (Supplemental Security Income) that may be available to your child: www.ssa.gov/ssi.

- www.SpecialOlympics.org

- StopBullying.gov provides strategies to prevent bullying and ways to build a safe school environment and community.

- Quackwatch.org is a website that focuses on health frauds, fads, trends, and fallacies.

END NOTES

1. "Why Act Early if You're Concerned about Development?" *Centers for Disease Control and Prevention,* https://www.cdc.gov/ncbddd/actearly/whyactearly.html (accessed September 21, 2023).

2. Caroline Myss, *Why People Don't Heal and How they Can* (New York: Harmony/Rodale, 2013), 15.

3. Elisabeth Kubler-Ross, *On Death and Dying* (New York: Macmillan, 1970).

4. Richard Paul Evans, *The Walk* (New York: Simon & Schuster, Inc., 2010), 217.

5. Viktor Frankl, *Man's Search for Meaning* (New York: Simon & Schuster, Inc., 1985), 86.

6. Lockett, Eleesha, "Your Guide to Situational Depression vs. Clinical Depression," *Healthline,* September 15, 2023 https://www.healthline.com/health/depression/situational-depression-vs-clinical-depression (accessed October 1, 2023).

7. Gibran, Kahil, *The Prophet* (New York: Alfred A..Knopf, 1923), 18. In public domain.

8. Moore, Lynn, *The Everything Parent's Guide to Children with Special Needs: A reassuring, informative guide to your child's well-being and happiness,* (New York: Simon & Schuster, 2009), 34-35.

9. Ann Gold Buscho, Ph.D., "Divorce and Special Needs Children," *Psychology Today,* February 28, 2023, https://www.psychologytoday.com/us/blog/a-better-divorce/202302/divorce-and-special-needs-children (accessed November 1, 2023).

10. "Can Babies Have Seizures in Utero?" *New Health Advisor,* https://www.newhealthadvisor.org/can-babies-have-seizures-in-utero.html (accessed November 16, 2023).

11. Morarji Peesay, M.D., "Cord Around the Neck Syndrome," *National Library of Medicine,* August 28, 2012, https://www.ncbi.nlm.nih.gov/pmc/articles/PMC3428673/ (accessed November 15, 2023).

12. Leslie Becker-Phelps, Ph.D., "When Guilt is Good … and When It's Misplaced," *Psychology Today,* September 10, 2012, https://www.psychologytoday.com/us/blog/making-change/201209/when-guilt-is-good-and-when-its-misplaced (accessed November 17, 2023).

13. Dodinsky, *In the Garden of Thoughts* (Naperville, IL: Sourcebooks, 2012).

14. Gračanin, A., Bylsma, L. M., & Vingerhoets, A. J. J. M., "Is Crying a Self-Soothing Behavior?" *Frontiers in Psychology* 5 (502), May 2014, https://www.researchgate.net/publication/262664292, (accessed October 5, 2023).

15. Buck, Pearl S. (Pearl Sydenstricker). *The Child Who Never Grew* (New York: Creative Media Partners, LLC, 2021), 33. In public domain.

16. "How Much Sleep Do You Really Need?" *National Sleep Foundation,* October 1, 2020, https://www.thensf.org/how-many-hours-of-sleep-do-you-really-need/ (accessed September 23, 2023).

17. Newsom, Rob, "Depression and Sleep," *Sleep Foundation,* November 16, 2023, https://www.sleepfoundation.org/mental-health/depression-and-sleep (accessed September 23, 2023).

18. Sarris, J., et al, "Personal View: Nutritional Medicine as Mainstream in Psychiatry," *The Lancet Psychiatry,* 2015, https://www.thelancet.com/journals/lanpsy/article/PIIS2215-0366(14)00051-0/fulltext (accessed November 1, 2023).

19. Pattemore, Chantelle "Nine Foods that Could Help You Manage Depression," *PsychCentral,* July 28, 2021, https://psychcentral.com/depression/foods-to-help-you-manage-depression#beneficial-foods (accessed November 1, 2023).

20. Moore, Lynn, *The Everything Parent's Guide to Children with Special Needs: A reassuring, informative guide to your child's well-being and happiness,* (New York: Simon & Schuster, 2009), 33.

21. befree, https://befreeco.com/pages/about (accessed January 2024).

22. Manguarian, Glenn E., "Realizing What You're Made Of," *Harvard Business Review's 10 Must Reads On Mental Toughness* (Boston: Harvard Business Review Press, 2018), 97-106.

23. Bombeck, Erma, *Motherhood, the Second Oldest Profession* (New York: McGraw-Hill, 1983), 70.

ACKNOWLEDGMENTS

First of all, I want to thank my daughter Kathryn Lauren Grady for being born to me. I will forever be grateful for the journey of a lifetime she placed me on. Also, this book wouldn't have been possible without Kathryn's entourage, the village of mainly women who cared for her in so many different ways, especially her beloved care provider, Novelita Domdom, and her dear family who embraced Kathryn as one of their own for 23 years. I also want to express tremendous gratitude for my own entourage who were there for me during Kathryn's last days, especially Mike and Beav Nace who opened their home for me in San Diego and welcomed me as family.

A special thank you to my Goal Sister Diane who has been listening to me say for the past 20 years that I wanted to write a book, my beloved friends Jim and Randy Weiss who read my manuscript and offered valuable feedback, and to my sixth-grade teacher, Mr. Trochim who encouraged me to be a writer after I won the sixth-grade writing contest!

I offer a huge thank you to Shane Crabtree at Clovercroft Publishing for helping me make my lifelong dream of being a published author come true, and to the very best copy editor in the world – Ann Tatlock.

I have enormous gratitude for my heroes, Dawn Patrice Garrett, John Pratt, and Vanessa McNear, for sharing their stories of their own unplanned journeys. They all make me want to be a better person.

Lastly, I will never forget Kit Keppler and Randy Herman. They were Kathryn's very best friends.

Kathryn enjoying one of her car rides to
Coronado and Imperial Beach — April 19, 2023

ABOUT THE AUTHOR

Janet Kelly has been a freelance writer for more than 20 years. *The Unplanned Journey* is her first book. When her daughter Kathryn was born with profound brain damage in 1991, she feared she would need to abandon any hope for her own personal goals or freedom. As Janet shares in her book, she learned to modify her new life to meet her needs as well as the needs of both of her daughters. Today, she is a full-time flight attendant and licensed esthetician with her own line of natural skin care. She wrote this book to provide other parents with the hope, comfort, and practical tips she wished someone had passed down to her all those years ago. Janet lives in Louisville, Kentucky, next door to her firstborn daughter Ann, grandson Tristin, and their ever-expanding family of dogs and cats.